rebel lives **sacco & vanzetti** rebel lives **sacco & vanzetti**

rebel lives, a fresh new series of inexpensive, accessible and provocative books unearthing the rebel histories of some familiar figures and introducing some lesser-known rebels

rebel lives, selections of writings by and about remarkable women and men whose radicalism has been concealed or forgotten. Edited and introduced by activists and researchers around the world, the series presents stirring accounts of race, class and gender rebellion

rebel lives does not seek to canonize its subjects as perfect political models, visionaries or martyrs but to make available the ideas and stories of imperfect revolutionary human beings to a new generation of readers and aspiring rebels

sacco & vanzetti

edited by John Davis

Ocean Press
Melbourne ■ New York
www.oceanbooks.com.au

Cover design by Sean Walsh and Meaghan Barbuto

Copyright © 2004 Ocean Press

ISBN: 1-876175-85-0
Library of Congress Control No: 2003112294
First Printed in Australia: 2004

Published by Ocean Press

Australia: GPO Box 3279, Melbourne, Victoria 3001, Australia
Fax: (61-3) 9329 5040 Tel: (61-3) 9326 4280
E-mail: info@oceanbooks.com.au

USA: PO Box 1186, Old Chelsea Stn., New York, NY 10113-1186, USA

Ocean Press Distributors:

United States and Canada: **Consortium Book Sales and Distribution**
Tel: 1-800-283-3572   www.cbsd.com

Britain and Europe: **Pluto Books**
E-mail: pluto@plutobooks.com

Australia and New Zealand: **Palgrave Macmillan**
E-mail: customer.service@macmillan.com.au

Cuba and Latin America: **Ocean Press**
E-mail: oceanhav@enet.cu

www.oceanbooks.com.au

contents

introduction

the trial of the century

On April 15, 1920, the small town of South Braintree, Massachusetts, had its quiet air shattered by the sound of gunfire and the roar of a car engine. A paymaster and his guard from the nearby Slater & Morrill Shoe Company lay dead in the street, the $16,000 payroll they had been carrying disappearing into the distance in a car, which was also whisking the two gunmen away from the scene. Though the crime was brutal, it was unremarkable, an all too regular occurrence as the world struggled to recover from World War I; initially the story barely rated a mention beyond the local press. Within a year it was to become "the trial of the century."

Three weeks later, two Italian immigrants and avowed anarchists, Nicola Sacco, a skilled shoemaker, and Bartolomeo Vanzetti, a fish-peddler, were arrested on a street car in Brockton, Massachusetts, and charged with the murders. Antiradical and anti-immigrant hysteria was sweeping the country, and the court case stumbled past inconclusive evidence to focus on Sacco and Vanzetti's anarchist views and draft-dodging. In what the American Federation of Labor called a "ghastly miscarriage of justice," they were sentenced to death. Seven years of court cases followed, demonstrations exploded across the United States, Europe and South America, and the politically motivated persecution of two unknown anarchists became an international cause célèbre.

If the ruling elite of Massachusetts felt that the execution of the two immigrants would put an end to the case, they were wrong. It has since inspired generations of activists, radicals, intellectuals, poets, writers and artists, some of whose work appears here. From the publication of Sacco and Vanzetti's letters to Ben Shahn's paintings *The Passion of Sacco and Vanzetti*; from Woody Guthrie's protest songs about the two political prisoners to the plethora of legal reviews that still regularly appear; from Joan Baez's music to Governor Michael Dukakis' 1977 proclamation that the men did not receive a fair trial; and through the global demonstrations and gatherings that mark the anniversary of their death every year, it has truly proved to be the case that will not die.

Today's catch-cry is: "Either you are with us or you are with the terrorists." Arabs have replaced Italians as the objects of suspicion, radicals are quickly labelled terrorists, and Sacco and Vanzetti's story is still powerfully resonant.

"did you see what I did to those anarchistic bastards the other day?"

For Italian anarchists, the United States of 1920 was a hostile place. In November 1919 Attorney General A. Mitchell Palmer launched a series of raids against labor and communist organizations, and immigrants, resulting in 10,000 arrests. Particular targets of these raids were "aliens," described by President Woodrow Wilson in 1915 as "hyphenated Americans [who have] poured the poison of disloyalty into the very arteries of our national life..." This witch-hunt resulted in the arrest and deportation of around 800 "noncitizens" and suspected radicals, including Emma Goldman and Alexander Berkman. Hoping that anti-immigrant hysteria and paranoia would win him the presidency, Palmer stated: "Out of the sly and crafty eyes of many of them leap cupidity, cruelty, insanity and crime; from their lopsided faces, sloping brows and misshapen features may be recognized the unmistakable criminal type."

But Sacco and Vanzetti were not just immigrants, they were also anarchists, "the radical of the radical" as Vanzetti would later say, and as such faced the greatest prejudices of a nation immersed in Red Scare hysteria. Indeed, after denying a motion for a new trial, Judge Thayer was quoted in an affidavit by Dartmouth Professor James Richardson as saying in 1924, "Did you see what I did to those anarchistic bastards the other day? That will hold them for a while."

When both men were arrested, they were carrying arms, and lied upon questioning. They believed they had been arrested for being radicals and immigrants, not murderers. These lies were particularly damaging to their legal defense, and were described by Judge Thayer as "consciousness of guilt as murderers or as slackers and radicals."

According to Felix Frankfurter, a professor of law at Harvard, the jury was selected "by sheriffs' deputies from Masonic gatherings and from persons whom the deputies deemed 'representative citizens,' 'substantial' and 'intelligent,'" and was headed by a foreman, Walter Ripley, who had commented to a friend prior to the trial, "Damn them, they ought to hang them anyway!" The scene was further set when Thayer directed the jury to "be loyal to the government," and "to seek courage in your deliberations such as was typified by the American soldier as he fought and gave up his life on the battlefields of France." The judge knew that Sacco and Vanzetti had escaped conscription by traveling to Mexico in 1916, and when District Attorney Frederick G. Katzmann gained an admission of their flight and further "confession" that they were atheists, the jury was well primed.

Katzmann's prosecution of the men was ruthless, withholding evidence from the jury and, assisted by the FBI, badgering and bullying witnesses. Historian Paul Avrich points out, "he played on the emotions of the jurors, arousing their deepest prejudices against the accused. Sacco and Vanzetti were armed at the time of their arrest; they were foreigners, atheists, anarchists. This overclouded all judgment."

Prosecution witnesses were repeatedly discredited under cross-examination and strong alibis for the defendants were provided by a number of witnesses. All of this, however, had little impact.

Despite his best efforts, their case wasn't helped by their original defense lawyer Fred H. Moore. As a "professional defender of radicals," a West Coast lawyer and someone unfamiliar with the intricacies of the Massachusetts bar, Moore found that the hostility directed toward his clients was also directed against him as an outsider. This eventually led to differences of opinion between the Defense Committee and Moore about how to proceed with the appeals process, and he was replaced by William G. Thompson in October 1923.

Yet apart from the legal maneuvering and horrific prejudice, Sacco and Vanzetti's story is also the story of two working people.

a good shoemaker and a poor fish-peddler

While Sacco and Vanzetti shared the same love of anarchism and met as members of a small group of anarchists under the influence of Luigi Galleani, the men had led very different lives.

Nicola Sacco was born in the southern Italian town of Torre-maggiorre on April 22, 1891, and worked for many years in his father's vineyard. He emigrated to the United States in 1908 at the age of 17, and the following year found work in the Milford Shoe Company. Sacco was respected for the quality and speed of his work, and learned the trade of an edger at a night school for shoe workers at the Three-K Shoe Company. He returned to the Three-K factory in Milford after avoiding the draft by fleeing to Mexico in 1916. He was trusted enough to become nightwatchman of the building at the request of the factory owner Michael F. Kelley, who always maintained that Sacco was incapable of committing the crime. "A man who is in his garden at 4 o'clock in the morning and at the factory at 7 o'clock," Kelley argued, "and in his garden again after supper and until nine and 10 at night, carrying water and raising vegetables beyond his own needs which he would bring to me to give to the poor — that man is not a 'holdup man.'"

Sacco arrived in the United States as a committed Italian republican but soon became an anarchist. He participated in a number of strikes at the Milford Shoe Company and was discovered by Kelley distributing radical literature at the Three-K factory. Kelley simply counseled him that there "was no money in it."

Sacco married in 1912 and had a son, Dante, in 1913. His daughter, Ines, was born after his arrest in 1920.

Bartolomeo Vanzetti was from Villafalletto, in the industrial north of Italy. He was born on June 11, 1888, to a family which was both middle class and devoutly Catholic. He went to school until the age of 13, when his father sent him to the city of Cuneo to become a baker. It was here, Vanzetti writes, that he tasted "for the first time, the flavor of hard, relentless labor." After six years and numerous jobs, he returned home to Villafalletto, seriously ill. His mother cared for him but then she died; this affected Vanzetti deeply. He left Italy not long after, on June 9, 1908. He was 20 years old.

While Sacco settled quickly into his new life among the Italian community in the United States, raising a family, saving money, tending his garden and furthering his involvement in the radical movement, Vanzetti became part of an army of itinerant workers criss-crossing the country in search of work. He was working as a fish-peddler when he was arrested in 1920.

Vanzetti was something of a philosopher and during his time working odd jobs in Springfield and Meriden he "learned that class consciousness was not a phrase invented by propagandists, but was a real, vital force, and that those who felt its significance were no longer beasts of burden, but human beings." He was an avid reader and during his imprisonment furthered his own education considerably. Many of the letters included here offer an insight into the mind of someone described by novelist Frederick Lewis Allen as "clearly a remarkable man — an intellectual of noble character, a philosophical anarchist of a type which it seemed impossible to associate with a pay-roll murder," and by columnist Heywood Broun as "one of the great men of the day."

It was perhaps sheer intellectual discipline and force of will that saw Vanzetti through the first four years of his detention, until suspected stomach ulcers weakened his resolve and in 1925 he spent a short period in Bridgewater Hospital for the Criminally Insane.

Sacco, with only a limited grasp of English, did not fare so well, spending longer periods in the hospital. It was not until 1922 that he asked for an English dictionary and wrote his first letter. His correspondence included here gives some insight into his frame of mind throughout the following years. While Vanzetti often displayed optimism at new developments in the appeals process and in the possibility that the working class would unite to free them, Sacco remained convinced that they would be executed regardless. In his final statement to the court upon sentencing, he said: "I know the sentence will be between two classes, the oppressed class and the rich class, and there will be always collision between one and the other. We fraternize the people with the books, with the literature. You persecute the people, tyrannize them and kill them." Sacco's letter to Cerise Jack, a member of the New England Civil Liberties Committee, in which he recounts a dream where he is killed imploring battling workers and soldiers to unite, displays an almost martyr-like quality and an adherence to a pragmatically pessimistic outlook. This contrasts with Vanzetti's more idealistic approach.

Along with this idealism, Vanzetti promoted a practical anarchism. At one point he exclaimed, "Both Nick and I are anarchists, the radical of the radical — the black cats, the terrors of many, of all the bigots, exploitators, charlatans, fakers and oppressors…" So while journalist and long-time supporter of the pair, Gardner Jackson, described "an aura of complete calm… and spirituality" surrounding Vanzetti, Paul Avrich suggests that "far from being the innocuous dreamers so often depicted by their supporters, they belonged… to a branch of the anarchist movement which preached insurrectionary violence and armed retaliation, including the use of dynamite and assassination."

save them for your honor

Sinclair wasn't the only literary figure to be affected by the case. A whole generation of writers, poets and artists became informed and were radicalized because, as Edmund Wilson pointed out in 1928, "it revealed the whole anatomy of American life, with all its classes and points of view and all their relations, and it raised almost every fundamental question of our political and social system."

Novelist John Dos Passos, for example, was involved in the Defense Committee for a number of years and wrote the committee's *Plea For The Defense* (included here). He also wrote extensive literary works inspired by the case, including the epic three volume fiction *U.S.A.* and the stream of consciousness montage, *The Camera Eye (50)*, in which he turns Palmer's anti-immigrant rhetoric on its head: "America our nation has been beaten by strangers who have turned our language inside out who have taken the clean words our fathers spoke and made them slimy and foul."

But the case affected more than those who were directly involved. Artist Ben Shahn, who painted a series of paintings titled *The Passion of Sacco and Vanzetti*, remarked in 1944:

> I had seen all the right pictures and read all the right books:
> Vollard, Meier-Graefe, David Hume. But still it didn't add up to
> anything. Then I got to thinking about the Sacco-Vanzetti case.
> They'd been electrocuted in 1927, and in Europe, of course,
> I'd seen all the demonstrations against the trial — a lot more
> than there were over here. Ever since I could remember I'd
> wished that I'd been lucky enough to be alive at a great time
> — when something big was going on, like the Crucifixion. And
> suddenly realized I was! Here I was living through another
> crucifixion. Here was something to paint!

Ironically, the religious connotations of words such as "Passion"
and "Crucifixion" angered many who had been involved in the
campaign to save the men, including some communist groups
who felt it was an insult to the anarchist principles of "no gods,
no masters."

Artists like George Grosz and George Biddle also contributed
work, alongside many political cartoonists whose illustrations
appeared in many liberal and radical publications.

Other luminaries joined the fight for justice. H.G. Wells, whose
1927 piece "The Proposed Murder of Two Radicals," which eventually appeared in his book of essays *The Way The World is Going*
after being denied publication in most of the U.S. press, is included
here, as is suffragist Elizabeth Glendower Evans's *New Republic*
article, "Foreigners," one of the earliest commentaries on the
case. Published that same year and included here is French
writer Anatole France's, "To the People of America," a plea which
finishes with: "Save them for your honor, for the honor of your
children and of all the generations yet unborn."

In fact, intellectuals and radicals in Europe played a major
role in publicizing the plight of the two Italian political prisoners
and the obvious miscarriage of justice. Philosopher Bertrand
Russell led the campaign in Britain claiming, "I am forced to

conclude that they were condemned on account of their political opinions and that men [who] ought to have known better allowed themselves to express misleading views as to the evidence because they held that men with such opinions have no right to live." Russell was so successful that at the height of the campaign a large number of British members of parliament spoke up in support of Sacco and Vanzetti, and former Prime Minister Ramsay MacDonald was quoted as saying, "This whole affair is too terrible; I hope the reputation of the United Sates will be saved the horror of this execution."

Newspapers and magazines around the world reported mass gatherings and riots in countries such as Germany, Austria, France and Italy. Mussolini apparently pleaded on behalf of the two men, though there is evidence to suggest that a conversation took place between the Italian and U.S. governments where Mussolini praised the United States' handling of the two anarchists and thanked them for saving him the burden of their deportation.

Anarchist Emma Goldman wrote and lectured on the topic extensively, including an impassioned article co-written with Alexander Berkman, written two years after their "legal murder." Back in the United States, socialist leader Eugene V. Debs was in regular contact with Sacco and Vanzetti, as can be seen by letters written to him provided here. Sacco and Vanzetti recognized the importance of solidarity as expressed in these letters, despite some ideological differences. Upon his release from jail in 1921, Debs donated his $5 "freedom payment" to their defense fund. Mother Jones exclaimed, "They'll never hang them," before learning of their fate, and Helen Keller and Charlie Chaplin took a vocal interest in the plight of the two political prisoners.

The Sacco and Vanzetti case brought together anarchists, communists and immigrants, in Massachusetts and around the world. Communist journalist James P. Cannon commented extensively on the case and called for political unity around the defense campaign: "We may have different opinions on many problems;

but there is one thing we have become sure of in these seven years... we have become convinced that Sacco and Vanzetti... are innocent of any crime except that of being rebels against the capitalist exploitation of the masses." Hundreds of thousands of workers attended meetings on the issue across the United States, resulting in heavy police repression and hundreds of arrests.

In the decades that have passed since Sacco and Vanzetti went to the electric chair, their case has continued to resonate. At various stages in history it has served to inform us that while the nature of repression and struggle remains essentially the same, we can draw hope and courage from two men who described themselves as "a good shoemaker and a poor fish-peddler," who died for their beliefs. The belief that we can create a world free from poverty and exploitation. The belief that another world is possible.

As Vanzetti himself said:

> If it had not been for these thing, I might have live out my life talking at street corners to scorning men. I might have die, unmarked, unknown a failure. Now we are not a failure. This is our career and our triumph. Never in our full life could we hope to do such work for tolerance, for justice, for mans understanding of man as now we do by accident. Our words — our lives — our pains nothing! The taking of our lives — Lives of a good shoemaker and a poor fish-peddler — All! That last moment belongs to us — That agony is our triumph!

notes on spelling and grammar

The spelling and grammar in the letters and quotes from Sacco and Vanzetti have been left as they were found. All other material has been altered to address U.S. styling.

The intention is to allow the reader some understanding of the frustrations the two political prisoners must have felt trying to express themselves in a language they were not fluent in.

part one:

The Shoemaker and the Fish-Peddler

The Words of Sacco and Vanzetti

Ben Shahn

from his 1932 series of paintings,
The Passion of Sacco and Vanzetti

Vanzetti to Alfonsina Brini

whose house he was living in when arrested.

January 10, 1921
Charlestown Prison

Dear Alfonsina,

I had received your letter dated January 6 to 21. I heartily laughed to hear that the fingernails of the little cat have scratched the Zora's nose, and I continue to laugh everytime I think about it. Surely it is a good lesson not only for Zora and other child, but for mankind. The little cat knows very well that it has a sharped nails, and that when a little girl molests it, it is enough to scratch a little her nose for be let free. People too has sharp finger-nails, and the noses [of] tyrants and oppressors is make of flesh too, but it look tho the people ignored this notion. Oh how much less sorrowness and misery would be among the mortals if they know just what a little cat knows. As for Zora, I know that she loves the cat, and is not cruel amongst it, but she played with it too much violently and insistently, and so hurts and troubles it, with the well merited consequences that she knows now pretty well. I am sorry for her nose, but when I thought that the cat had anticipated my advice, I can't help but laugh. Tell Beltrando that I received his callender; much oblige to him. I hear that the woolen mill has stopped to work, and you are without job. Certainly, owed to the high price of everything, and your familiar circumstances, it shall trouble you. But take it easy. After all we cannot become rich by the work of our arms... Take this opportunity to enjoy sunshine and open air...

I am glad for your good news. I too feel very well. Thanks for all.

Kisses to the children, best regards to Vincenzo and all those who love me. Cheer up, be careful for your health.

P.S. One more order: If you have yet that callender with the world map, send it to me. I shall smile, in spite of the chain, in looking our gradual World's conquest.

Vanzetti to socialist leader Eugene V. Debs

September 29, 1923
Charlestown Prison

Dear Comrade E. Debs,
It is long time, since your unforgettable visit to me, that I am wishing to write to you.

I have told to one of the noblest women of this nation that I am ashamed to have been unable to speak to you; and she answered "Do not whorry of it, E. Debs understan it." And, as prove, she told me a similar case in the life of her mother, who has understood and appreciated the silence of a friend. I realize that you have understood me — but, nevertheless I wished, I wish to express to you my gratitude, my respect and my love.

As you know, I belong to the extreme anarchistic school — but maybe you ignore the admiration and affection that we, Italian anarchists, have for you — or, rather, that you won from us.

You and Lucy Parson[s] are the two American for whose personal acquaintance I have longed for many years. Now I have the pleasure to know both of you.

Once, when living in Farrel, P. I have heard that you would have come to speak in Charlestown, O. All the Italian anarchists of the neighborhood were there, waiting for you. But a telegram came, and told your impossibility to reach the city. So I have had to wait many years before to see you. And I must confess that when I saw you I went near to cry.

You and I belong to different schools of socialism — but you are my teacher.

I do not vote, but I would trust unto you the sacrest and dearest things of the life.

Because you have superated this age, arose above the narrow limits of parties and of sects, and masterly preach by exemples.

I am firmly convinced that the results of the human convivence: miseries, darkness and death, or health, light, happiness and life, are more determined by the qualities and the deeds of the individuals than by parties' and sets' programs and creeds. And I am positive that if a minority would follow your (practical) example the reality of the to-morrow would be above the dreams of many dreamers.

I expect to be bring in Court next Monday; also, have some letters to be wrote; and wish to write an article before to-morrow night: for these reasons I must close this letter, praying you to exscuse my poor English and to accept my sincere sentiments.

Your, with great heart,
Bartolomeo V

Vanzetti to suffragette Elizabeth Glendower Evans

*of Brookline, Massachusetts, who corresponded with
both men throughout their imprisonment.*

Winter, 1923
Charlestown Prison

Dear Mrs. Evans,

When the hour given for the visit is past I feel to have more to say
than at the beginning of it, and so it happen that I think always a
long time upon what was left to be said.

Undoubtedly the great sources of Russian Revolution troubles
are of extern origin; others of natural origin by which man's power
is overwhelmed; but some must be in the nature of all those human acts which constitute a Revolution. I fear, I am rather almost
sure that a great sabotage is practised against the new order.
Now, the only way to be victorious is to eliminate the cause
which determined any hostil deed against the revolution. The
confidence of the [Russian] people in a violent punishment
[against the rest of the world], operated by a new constitutional
force, is such a folly that lead to an abyss; and the best result of
a revolution, I mean that mental and moral improvement that
every real worthy revolution should operate over the people, will
so be destroyed.

But many things one could say about this subject, and be-
sides, the work of the critic is always the easy one: so I return
on the old subject "Morals." Man call moral everything that is
favorable to conservation of life, to happiness of the individual, as
well of the race, and these things are virtues and justice. For this
reason, I cannot believe in those philosophers, who speaking of
morals, tell me about a categoric order, a revelation, an abstract
principle, and so on.

For me, the moral sense come from the strongest instincts of every living being. I mean the instincts of conservation and happiness, which as soon as the intelligence come, generates a third instinct, the love of the race. As soon as any intelligent creatures begin a social life they are compelled to social duties: hence the notion of what is just and what is unjust, of what is good and what is evil. So, we can say that morals, as well as everything else made by man, has the purpose of conservation and happiness. That is why he who said that the fundamental nature of morals do not change, was right, and that is the reason why men breaks a moral relation to anythings or person as soon he stops believeing in their goodness and justice. And this is why every new idea that mark a progress has in itself a superior moral.

What Kropotkin said in his Anarchist Moral: "Do to others what you would wish that the others should do to you, in the same circumstances," can be the basis of the morals. Of course, many comrades had criticised him, but my little I, believe him very near to the reason. Nothing new in this, save a little modification which not only command to not do unjust things, but command also to do good. And this is progress. Every normal persons can be in accord.

The trouble and the differences begin when the moral values of our present institutions, of our social contract, of our customs are put in discussion. And more complications arise when we treat of details of the life, of the relativeness and absoluteness of it, because we all are individual, and, what is more important, determined creatures leaded in life by an influence of our personal life, amid a perpetual conflict between the mind and the heart.

But we have instincts that lead us, and intelligence that serves them, and after all, a nature fundamentally equal. Those things would be enough if man should not be susceptible of degeneration, as soon as he left his natural way of life. Here we face a gigantic problem; not a letter but a book will be necessary to resolve or better to prospect it.

Before concluding, I put to myself a question, and answer to it. What is the good, and what is the evil? Till now from the greatest luminaries to the last dagoes wandering over the land, the idea is "All what help me is the good, all the rest is the evil." It is as Gorki said about the moral of the savage, and it run as follows: "If I steal the wife of my neighbor that is the good; if my neighbor steals my wife that is the evil." To be exact there are many and enough of moral principles abstractly true, but they are vitiated by their application.

The anarchist go ahead and says: All what is help to me without hurt the others is good; all what help the others without hurting me is good also, all the rest is evil. He look for his liberty in the liberty of all, for his happiness in the happiness of all, for his welfare in the universal welfare. I am with him.

Well, I perceive I have been very incomplete and inexact in my words, but, there are no pretention in them. They arise out of the intention of reveal my thought and exercising in English language. I begun to read the bible!

Vanzetti to Alice Stone Blackwell

of Boston, Massachusetts, who was active in
various feminist and suffragette groups.

February 27, 1924
Charlestown Prison

Dear Comrade Blackwell,
Yours of the 23rd has reached me. You are right. Neither do I expect any good from that letter to the judge. I have never expected, nor do I expect anything from him, other than some ten thousand volts divided in few times; some meters of cheap board and 4x7x8 feet hole in the ground.

No matter how much sympathy I try to bestow upon him, or with how much understanding I try to judge his actions; I only and alone can see him a self-conceited narrow-minded little tyrant, believing himself to be just and believing his utterly unjust and unnecessary social office to be a necessity and a good. He is a bigot, and therefore, cruel. At the time of our arrest and trials, his peers were seeing red all around, and he saw red more than his peers.

He was ready to kill us even before the trials, for he deadly hates the subversive, and he believed to have become judge of the State Supreme Court by eliminating us via Law. For he knows that the servants of Capital were always remunerated by the Bosses for a crusifixion of some rebel or lover.

I do not know if his conduct during the trial was determined by his preconceptions, hate and ignorance, or if he consciously murdered us by details of bad faith, double paying, simulation, etc. I know that he did it. I know that even now he does not want to give us another trial though he could not deny it. And this is why he delays so much to give the answer...

And if I am wrong, if according to his own standard, he is fair, if he wishes to be just, ('til now he is very unjust) then he could be hurt by my letter, but also enlightened. And if he would not forgive the crude defense of a man extremely wronged, then, not even a sparrow would I submit to him as arbiter.

An almost centennial struggle against every form of exploitation, oppression and fraud, taught us that "the wolf eats him who makes himself a sheep."

I am not sure, but I believe, that there are no pamphlets in Italian language, which treat with detail the case. This is the second reason of my letter and the third reason is, my wish to say what no one else can say — silence would be cowardness — and treat the case accordingly to my own criterions. This may hurt me, but will help the Cause. Otherwise, if it means a life sentence, I prefer to be burnt away once and for all, and I also know that those in height, upon the back and the heads of the slaves, are against me...

There is no spirit of sacrifice in this deed. I simply realize to be in merciless hands, and do my utmost to say to my enemy that he is wrong. In a way that helps the cause. The great one, not the small. My only hope remains in the solidarity of friends and comrades and of the workers. After having spent $200,000, we are still at the beginning. The work of the lawyers are useless before the law.

It has helped only because they brought the fact to the conscience and consciousness of the People. That is why Nick and I were not yet roasted. Authority, Power and Privilege would not last a day upon the face of the earth, were it not because those who possess them and those who prostitute their arms to their defense do suppress, repress, mercilessly and inescapable every efforts of liberations of each and all the rebels.

I abhor useless violence. I would my blood to prevent the sheading of blood, but neither the abyss nor the earth, nor the heavens, have a law which condemns the self-defense. Not every woman has sacrificed to bring forth one more ruffian, idiot or coward to the world. There are yet some men. And if the tragedy is compelled to us, who knows; who knows if to speak now is not my duty?

The champion of life and of the liberty should not yield before the death. The struggle for the liberty, between the oppressor and the oppressed, shall continue beyond the life, beyond the graves. I know what they have done and are doing to me and to thousands of others, rebels and lovers. And I know that they are and will always be against us. I know the millions of youth that they slandered, the virgins that they have torn in the breast; the millions of wives that they have widowed; the millions of bastards that they let to miasma of the gutter, or grown to the fratricide. I know the old fathers and mothers whom they killed by breaking their hearts; and all the children that they starved and are starving to death; and the hospitals and the crazy houses filled of their victims, irresponsible and semi-compelled to crime that they mercilessly executed or entombed alive. They have never had pity for our children, our women. Our dear, poor old fathers and mothers — and they will never have it.

The sorrow of their victims torture me in blood and spirit. As for me, I would forgive them, but I could not, for I would be a traitor of the race. Until not a man will be exploited or oppressed by another man, we will never bend the banner of freedom.

Are they not ready to do with other comrades what they are doing to us? Are they not more willing than ever to squeeze out the worker's blood for gold? Are they not preparing a greater war?

I will ask for revenge — I will tell them that I will die gladly by the hands of the hanger after having known to have been vindicated. I mean "eye for an eye, ear for an ear," and even more, since to win it is necessary that 100 enemies fall to each of us.

The only vengeance which could placate me is the realization of freedom, the great deliverance which would beneficiate all my friends as well as my enemies: All. But toll that, the struggle goes on, till we are breath to breath with the enemy fighting with short arms, till then to fight is our duty, our right, our necessity. For, one of the two. Either we must go on and win, or we must ask for armistice. And who will grant it to us? Since the enemy has no scruples nor pity, to ask pity of him is to encourage him to slander our fellows, to try to grant to him the immunity for his crimes against us; it would be as good as matricide.

The more I live, the more I suffer, the more I learn, the more I am inclined to forgive, to be generous, and that the violence as such does not resolve the problem of life. And the more I love and learn that "the right of all to violence does not go together with the liberty, but it begins when the liberty ends." The slave has the right and the duty to arise against his master. My supreme aim, that of the Anarchist is, "the complete elimination of violence from the rapports [relations]."

To be possible we must have freedom and justice. Now we have the opposite of them, because through errors and consequent aberrations, men have risen as tyrants, deceiters and exploiters of other men, believing to gain their personal, familiar and cast welfare by such deed. Through both tyranny and servitude, we have lost our capacity of liberty and we are making life evermore miserable, operating our own ante-distruction.

Since "only the liberty, or the struggle for liberty, may be school of liberty" and since mine is but self and racial defense, why should not I use the truth to defend myself? It is supremely sweet to me — my consciousness of superiority, of righteousness, to know that I can judge and that the future shall bow to me, the doomed, and curse my judges.

Well, I have said many things which I sincerely believe to be so. But there are surely some mistake! Who possesses the absolute, or even the absolute-relative truth? So your point of view may be right, and I also realized that you spoke exclusively for my own good.

Wisdom is not only comprehension, but also many other

faculties together; among which discrimination and sense of measure are prominent. I will try to be wise !!!!!! I will think it over and over again.

This month I have had no visits, a little mail, and waited in vain for Mr. Moore and company, Mrs. Evans and Mrs. V. Mac-Mechan...

Altogether, sometime, in my solitude, I think that the world is gradually forgetting this son of it, entombed alive. But, I will bear my cross. There are those who will never forget me...

P.S. I began to study arithmetic, and I find that my mind works in the same way. A Mathematic mind then? I asked it since I wonder that during 36 years no one else had perceived it, and the one who did it, fear to [do] me wrong.

Sacco to Cerise Jack

of Sharon, Massachusetts, who was part of the New England Civil Liberties Committee, visited the men in jail, and gave Sacco English lessons during the winter of 1923-24.

March 15, 1924
Dedham Jail

My Dear Friend Mrs. Jack,
It has been past a few day now that I had in my mind to write you a letter and I always try to find some good idea, but it was hard because the sky it has been covered for several day now with full of cloud; and you know that my most beauty idea I find by looking at the clear and blue sky...

So Wednesday night I went to sleep with idea to write you at first thing in morning but when I was into bed I begen to turn this way an the other way and I was try my best to sleep. So after while I fall sleep, enddid I do not know how long I been sleep when I was up again with a terrible dream... terrible I said yes, but beauty at same time, and here way it is. The dream it was develope in one place in mine camp of Pennsylvania state, and here it was a big large number of laborers in strike for better wages and the masses of workers they was impatient tired of long waiting, because the bos who own the col mine there threw out of the house a big number people, of poor mother and child and for the moment they were living under the tent in one concentration camp. But here the poor mother they was not pacific yet, because they know that they would soon send the soldiers to chase the mother out of the camp.

And so the big masse of the workers they was in complete revolt from the cruelty the bos of the mine. In this camp they were two or three speakers and every one of them they was used a kind and warm word for the freedom of the peeple. While the immensity of the work masses they were applauding the speakers, the soldiers comes with bayonet gun for chase the crowd, but after word they find out they was wrong because every one of the strikers they stand still like one man. And so the fight it was beginning, and while the fight was begin I jump upon a little hill in meddle of the crowd and I begin to say, Friend and comrade and brotherhood, not one of us is going to move a step, and who will try to move it will be vile and coward, here the fight is to go to finish. So I turn over toward the soldiers and I said, Brothers you will not fire on your own brothers just because they tell you to fire, no brothers, remember that everyone of us we have mother and child, and you know that we fight for freedom which is your freedom. We want one fatherland, one sole, one house, and better bread. So while I was finish to say that last word one of the soldiers fire toward me and the ball past through my heart, and while I was fall on ground with my right hand close to my heart I awake up with sweet dream! So when I was awake I had my right hand still tightly upon my heart like if it was hold back the speed of the beating of my heart. I turn over toward my window cell and through the shade of night I was looking at sky, and while look the stars it bright my face and the shadow soon disapear. Soon the idea it comes in my mind to write my dream to my dear teacher and for moment I thought that Fairhope, Alabama was to far away but the spirit, the voice the lesson of my dear and good friend and teacher Mrs. Jack it is remained in my heart and blessed my soul...

Vanzetti to Maude Pettyjohn
of Dayton, Washington.

April 10, 1925
Bridgewater Hospital for Criminally Insane

Dear Friend,
...I cannot share your confidence in "better government," because I do not believe in the government, any of them, since to me they can only differ in names from one another, and because we have witnessed the utterly failure of both the social-democrat governments in Germany, and the bolsheviki government in Russia.

At least, such is my honest and sad opinion. But I wholly share of your confidence in Co-operatives, and, what is more, in real co-operatives, free initiative, both individual and collective. Mutual aid and co-operation and co-operatives shall be the very base of a completely new social system, or else, nothing is accomplished...

But when you tell me that the only consolation you give to your complaining friends against economical difficulties, is "that the times will be much harder," then I cannot help but clap my hands in great approval. So much so, that it is but the truth. And not only in economy, but in life's problems this will be true.

We are galloping toward misery and wretchedness. Life grows miserable by each second, and he whom the gods have not yet wholly deprived of understanding, far from being surprised, should indeed wonder if it were not so, for, man is today his own greater enemy, and the slaves are, more than the powerful, the slave-keeper of themselves. Crucial truth for the libertarian, truth that drowns tears from our eyes, and curses from our heart, curses to those whom we would also deliver for their own sake...

Even before I came here, I was the cause of much disturbed fear; distrust of keepers and doctors who have their jobs, love them and believe me and my friends the worst and dangerous criminals. The higher of them the more jack-asses.

So it follows that I was kept in solitary confinement for five weeks, after which I was allowed to the dayroom, where it is forbidden to speak, and watched by eyes always. A few days after that I was admitted to the common table; knives and forks were taken off from circulation, and we compelled to use the fingers as table-tools. Meanwhile, every good day, the other patients were compelled to go into the yard, and I had to stay in. It is five years that I have been deprived of all that makes life worth living. Sunlight and open-air is what is greatly needed after five years of shadows and miasmatic dwelling.

So I kicked and I kicked: I want my rights, and I have the right of a daily hour in the open air. The State so splendidly framed us, cannot it give me any rights? Meanwhile, I began to perceive abuse and wrongs to the patients and, therefore, to protest and rebel. Were I alone, they would, for this, have me die within this wall. Well, after my protests, I was allowed to go into the yard; once a day, early in the morning, when none were there, and together with the biggest attendance. Thus, in three months, I went seven times into the yard, and only the seventh I stayed there one hour, all the other, less. I used to clean the floors, help the patients take off the dust, watering plants, etc., so that the head assistant proclaimed me to the doctors "his better patient." And yet they kept watching, fearing and distrusting me to the point that the head assistant said that I should write in English my letters to my sister, to which I answered in rhymes...

Vanzetti to Alice Stone Blackwell

of Boston, Massachusetts.

June 13, 1926
Charlestown Prison

Dear Comrade Blackwell,
Last Thursday, Mrs. Evans was here, and she gave me a copy of the *New Republic,* containing the editorial on our case, and indeed a splendid editorial. Oh, if everyone who wrote on our case would have had such a capacity and treated it so well as that writer, how much better it would have been for us. The indolence, the incapacity, the inexactness of those who have willingly or half-willingly wrote on our case, has always caused much disgust, and, often, indignation and wrath to me. I am sorry to say that the writings of the conservative or of the liberals have shown much more competence, sense of measure and of responsibility,

than those of the more near to me. The writings of our Eugene
Debs and those of the anarchist weekly *Fede* of Rome are the
better of all; and good ones have been written by our affines. Yet,
someone of our comrades made big errs and blunders. Thus the
truth is spoiled, the seriousness of the case destroyed together
with the trustings of the intelligent and impartial readers. What a
contrast with the perfect, superfine ability of our enemies. Of all
this I have spoken and lamented with one of the *The Masses*
staff who was here a few days ago.

For several weeks I received *Il Nuovo Mondo*, an anti-fascist
daily of New York, sustained by the American Clothing Amalga-
mated Union, and edited by the ex-Italian congressman, Vincenzo
Vacirca, a unitario-socialist. I must say the following, even if it
tears my heart. If we do not know to do better, we are doomed by
our incapacity to a perpetual vanquishment — we will ruin even
the most complete victory of a revolution brought first by other
historical factors than ourselves. That anti-fascism has in itself,
endemic, the fascism. It is as equivocous as that anti-clericalism
which consist in fighting the clergy by revealing the priest's sins
through pornografic expositions and in a false, unilateral historical
philosophy, which consist in a wrong and partisan interpretation
of the churches history. Equivocous as that atheism that affirms
itself with blasphemous bravados, with dogmatic criterion on the
creation and on the universe, with a trumpetting ignorance of the
human nature and a self-imposing simpleton philosophy. And I
could go on, on, and on.

Well, the *Nuovo Mondo* has talked a great deal about our
case, within these last few weeks. But, oh, how badly!... It was
most humiliating and painful to be compelled to recognize that
the facisti or philofacisti Italo-American *Progresso* and *Popolo*,
New York dailies, have shown more earnestness and intensity
of feeling in helping us, according to their character and thought
and skillful journalistic ability. Well, I take it easy and am more
displeased for the great than for my personal little cause...

That our framers and doomers might be afraid of punishment, it is well comprehensable. Moved by greed, hatred and prejudice, or compelled, they have determinedly acted against us and disposed to kill us. Being themselves actual murderers, they cannot help but to measure the others with themselves and to fear. And I not christian, am for vindication — but rather than to spill a single drop of innocent blood, I prefer to be electrocuted for a crime of which I am utterly innocent. In six years of wrong, abuses, outrages, persecution, revenges and of too slow murdering, none of our enemies have been touched. If they fear, the justification and the source of their fearing is in themselves...

Sacco to Eugene V. Debs

from Charlestown Prison.

October 20, 1926
Boston, Massachusetts

My Dear Debs,
The day of yesterday were so sad and gloomy, but this morning it seems more bright that ever; yes, it's so, because this morning just sooner I get up my eyes were turn toward the daylight, and upon the tops at the oak tree between the gold leaves, smillen, the old vegliant image of Eugene Debs in my eyes appear, and the affable smile of his noble face were telling me that he feel all better. Therefore, the appear of your dear image at my vision it was that, the guarder were telling me last night that their have read in the Boston newspaper that you were at the hospital badly

sick. So this morning my first thought was to sent you these few lines, for I know that it will relief you noble soul. Just as much as your unforgettable dearest letter they have and [unreadable] to relieve my soul.

I am so really ashame to say to you, dear comrade, courage! But however, you will be good to let me tell you that, more the once in the struggle lifetime and even when a man were lying in bet saving the good old courage, win victoriously the depressed state body. Therefore, I am merely thout it — by remind your old intrepid good spirit, would revive the life in you; and I hope from the bottom of my heart so see you sooner image your old and the young brother comrades (again), because they need the thought and the sincere radiant words from the sweet Voice of Euge Debs.

So, dear comrade, courage! Because before were pass at the eternity world, I want see you, kiss you and so tight you in meni embrace warmly.

Best wishes to you dear wife Theodore and all his family from all my dear household kiss from my little one join with most warmly and brotherly embrace.

Won and forever your faithful comrade
Ferdinando N. Sacco

Sacco's statement upon sentencing

April 9, 1927, Dedham Court House.

CLERK WORTHINGTON: Nicola Sacco, have you anything to say why sentence of death should not be passed upon you?

NICOLA SACCO: Yes, sir. I am no orator. It is not very familiar with me the English language, and as I know, as my friend has told me, my comrade Vanzetti will speak more long, so I thought to give him the chance.

I never knew, never heard, even read in history anything so cruel as this Court. After seven years prosecuting they still consider us guilty. And these gentle people here are arrayed with us in this court today.

I know the sentence will be between two classes, the oppressed class and the rich class, and there will be always collision between one and the other. We fraternize the people with the books, with the literature. You persecute the people, tyrannize them and kill them. We try the education of people always. You try to put a path between us and some other nationality that hates each other. That is why I am here today on this bench, for having been of the oppressed class. Well, you are the oppressor.

You know it, Judge Thayer — you know all my life, you know why I have been here, and after seven years that you have been persecuting me and my poor wife, and you still today sentence us to death. I would like to tell all my life, but what is the use? You know all about what I say before, that is, my comrade, will be talking, because he is more familiar with the language, and I will give him a chance. My comrade, the kind man to all the children, you sentenced him two times, in the Bridgewater case and the Dedham case, connected with me, and you know he is innocent.

You forget all this population that has been with us for seven years, to sympathize and give us all their energy and all their kindness. You do not care for them. Among that peoples and the comrades and the working class there is a big legion of intellectual people which have been with us for seven years, to not commit the iniquitous sentence, but still the Court goes ahead. And I want to thank you all, you peoples, my comrades who have been with me for seven years, with the Sacco Vanzetti case, and I will give my friend a chance.

I forget one thing which my comrade remember me. As I said before, Judge Thayer know all my life, and he know that I am never guilty, never — not yesterday, nor today, nor forever.

Vanzetti's statement upon sentencing

April 9, 1927, Dedham Court House.

CLERK WORTHINGTON: Bartolomeo Vanzetti, have you anything to say why sentence of death should not be passed upon you?

BARTOLOMEO VANZETTI: Yes. What I say is that I am innocent, not only of the Braintree crime, but also of the Bridgewater crime. That I am not only innocent of these two crimes, but in all my life I have never stolen and I have never killed and I have never spilled blood. That is what I want to say...

Well, I want to reach a little point further, and it is this, that not only have I not been trying to steal in Bridgewater, not only have I not been in Braintree to steal and kill and have never stolen or killed or spilt blood in all my life, not only have I struggled hard against crimes, but I have refused myself of what are considered the commodity and glories of life, the prides of a life of a good position, because in my consideration it is not right to exploit man. I have refused to go in business because I understand that business is a speculation on profit upon certain people that must depend upon the business man, and I do not consider that that is right and therefore I refuse to do that.

Now, I should say that I am not only innocent of all these things, not only have I never committed a real crime in my life — though some sins but not crimes — not only have I struggled all my life to eliminate crimes that the official law and the moral law condemns, but also the crime that the moral law and the official law sanction and sanctify — the exploitation and the oppression of the man by the man, and if there is a reason why I am here as a guilty man, if there is a reason why you in a few minutes can doom me, it is this reason and none else...

We were tried during a time whose character has now passed into history. I mean by that, a time when there was a hysteria of resentment and hate against the people of our principles, against the foreigner, against slackers, and it seems to me — rather, I am positive of it, that both you and Mr. Katzmann have done all what it were in your power in order to work out, in order to agitate still more the passion of the juror, the prejudice of the juror, against us...

Because the jury were hating us because we were against the war, and the jury don't know that it makes any difference between a man that is against the war because he believes that the war is unjust, because he hate no country, because he is a cosmopolitan, and a man that is against the war because he is in favor of the other country that fights against the country in which he is, and therefore a spy, an enemy, and he commits any crime in the country in which he is in behalf of the other country in order to serve the other country. We are not men of that kind. Nobody can say that we are German spies or spies of any kind.

Katzmann knows very well that. Katzmann knows that we were against the war because we did not believe in the purpose for which they say that the war was fought. We believed that the war is wrong, and we believe this more now after 10 years that we studied and observed and understood it day by day — the consequences and the result of the after war. We believe more now than ever that the war was wrong, and we are against war more now than ever, and I am glad to be on the doomed scaffold if I can say to mankind, "Look out; you are in a catacomb of the flower of mankind. For what? All that they say to you, all that they have promised to you — it was a lie, it was an illusion, it was a cheat, it was a fraud, it was a crime. They promised you liberty. Where is liberty? They promised you prosperity. Where is prosperity? They have promised you elevation. Where is the elevation?"

From the day that I went in Charlestown, the misfortunate, the population of Charlestown, has doubled in number. Where is the moral good that the war has given to the world? Where is the spiritual progress that we have achieved from the war? Where are the security of life, the security of the things that we possess for our necessity? Where are the respect for human life? Where are the respect and the admiration for the good characteristics and the good of the human nature? Never before the war as now have there been so many crimes, so much corruption, so much degeneration as there is now...

Well, I have already say that I not only am not guilty of these two crimes, but I never committed a crime in my life — I have never stolen and I have never killed and I have never spilt blood, and I have fought against crime, and I have fought and I have sacrificed myself even to eliminate the crimes that the law and the church legitimate and sanctify.

This is what I say: I would not wish to a dog or to a snake, to the most low and misfortunate creature of the earth — I would not wish to any of them what I have had to suffer for things that I am not guilty of. I am suffering because I am a radical and indeed I am a radical; I have suffered because I was an Italian, and indeed I am an Italian; I have suffered more for my family and for my beloved than for myself, but I am so convinced to be right that you can only kill me once but if you could execute me two times, and if I could be reborn two other times, I would live again to do what I have done already.

Sacco to his daughter Ines

then almost seven years old.

July 19, 1927
Charlestown State Prison

My Dear Ines,

I would like that you should understand what I am going to say to you, and I wish I could write you so plain, for I long so much to have you hear all the heart-beat eagerness of your father, for I love you so much as you are the dearest little beloved one.

It is quite hard indeed to make you understand in your young age, but I am going to try from the bottom of my heart to make you understand how dear you are to your father's soul. If I cannot succeed in doing that, I know that you will save this letter and read it over in future years to come and you will see and feel the same heart-beat affection as your father feels in writing it to you.

I will bring with me your little and so dearest letter and carry it right under my heart to the last day of my life. When I die, it will be buried with your father who loves you so much, as I do also your brother, Dante and holy dear mother.

You don't know Ines, how dear and great your letter was to your father. It is the most golden present that you could have given to me or that I could have wished for in these sad days.

It was the greatest treasure and sweetness in my struggling life that I could have lived with you and your brother Dante and your mother in a neat little farm, and learn all your sincere words and tender affection. Then in the summer-time to be sitting with you in the home nest under the oak tree shade — beginning to teach you of life and how to read and write, to see you running, laughing, crying and singing through the verdent fields picking the wild flowers here and there from one tree to another, and from the clear, vivid stream to your mother's embrace.

The same I have wished to see for other poor girls, and their brothers, happy with their mother and father as I dreamed for us — but it was not so and the nightmare of the lower classes saddened very badly your father's soul.

For the things of beauty and of good in this life, mother nature gave to us all, for the conquest and the joy of liberty. The men of this dying old society, they brutally have pulled me away from the embrace of your brother and your poor mother. But, in spite of all, the free spirit of your father's faith still survives, and I have lived for it and for the dream that some day I would have come back to life, to the embrace of your dear mother, among our friends and comrades again, but woe is me!

I know that you are good and surely you love your mother, Dante and all the beloved ones — and I am sure that you love me also a little, for I love you much and then so much. You do not know Ines, how often I think of you every day. You are in my heart, in my vision, in every angle of this sad walled cell, in the sky and everywhere my gaze rests.

Meantime, give my best paternal greetings to all the friends and comrades, and doubly so to our beloved ones. Love and kisses to your brother and mother.

With the most affectionate kiss and ineffable caress from him who loves you so much that he constantly thinks of you. Best warm greetings from Bartolo to you all.

Your Father

Vanzetti to Governor Alvan T. Fuller

six days before Fuller announced his decision on the findings of the special commission headed by Dr. Lawrence Lowell of Harvard University.

July 28, 1927
Charlestown Prison

...I am an Italian, a stranger in a foreign country, and my witnesses are the same kind of people. I am accused and convicted on the testimony of mostly American witnesses. Everything is against me — my race, my opinions and my humble occupation. I did not commit either of these crimes, and yet how am I ever going to show it if I and all my witnesses are not believed, merely because the police want to convict somebody, and get respectable Americans to testify against us? I suppose a great many Americans think that it is alright to stretch the truth a little to convict an anarchist; but I don't think they would think so if they were in my place. And if any of them were accused of crime in Italy, and tried before an Italian jury at a time when Americans were not very popular in Italy, I think they would realize the truth of what I have been trying to say...

Sacco to the Sacco-Vanzetti Defense Committee

August 4, 1927
Charlestown State Prison

My Dear Friends and Comrades,
From the death cell we are just inform from the defense committee that the governor Fuller he has decided to kill us August the 10th. We are not surprised for this news because we know the capitalist class hard without any mercy the good soldiers of the rivolution. We are proud for death and fall as all the anarchist can fall. It is up to you now, brothers, comrades! as I have tell you yesterday that you only that can save us, because we have never had faith in the governor for we have always know that the gov. Fuller, Thayer and Katzmann are the murder.

My warm fraternal regards to all,
Nicola Sacco

Sacco to his son Dante

then approximately 14 years old.

August 18, 1927
Charlestown State Prison

My Dear Son and Companion,
Since the day I saw you last I had always the idea to write you this letter, but the length of my hunger strike and the thought I might not be able to explain myself, made me put it off all this time.

The other day, I ended my hunger strike and just as soon as I did that I thought of you to write to you, but I find that I did not have enough strength and I cannot finish it at one time. However, I want to get it down in any way before they take us again to the death house, because it is my conviction that just as soon as the court refuses a new trial to us they will take us there. And between Friday and Monday, if nothing happens, they will electrocute us right after midnight, on August 22nd. Therefore, here I am, right with you with love and with open heart as ever I was yesterday.

I never thought that our inseparable life could be separated, but the thought of seven dolorous years makes it seem it did come, but then it has not changed really the unrest and the heart-beat of affection. That has remained as it was. More. I say that our ineffable affection reciprocal, is today more than any other time, of course. That is not only a great deal but it is grand because you can see the real brotherly love, not only in joy but also and more in the struggle of suffering. Remember this, Dante. We have demonstrated this, and modesty apart, we are proud of it.

Much we have suffered during this long Calvary. We protest

today as we protested yesterday. We protest always for our freedom.

If I stopped hunger strike the other day, it was because there was no more sign of life in me. Because I protested with my hunger strike yesterday as today I protest for life and not for death.

I sacrificed because I wanted to come back to the embrace of your dear little sister Ines and your mother and all the beloved friends and comrades of life and not death. So Son, today life begins to revive slow and calm, but yet without horizon and always with sadness and visions of death.

Well, my dear boy, after your mother had talked to me so much and I had dreamed of you day and night, how joyful it was to see you at last. To have talked with you like we used to in the days — in those days. Much I told you on that visit and more I wanted to say, but I saw that you will remain the same affectionate boy, faithful to your mother who loves you so much, and I did not want to hurt your sensibilities any longer, because I am sure that you will continue to be the same boy and remember what I have told you. I knew that and what here I am going to tell you will touch your sensibilities, but don't cry Dante, because many tears have been wasted, as your mother's have been wasted for seven years, and never did any good. So, Son, instead of crying, be strong, so as to be able to comfort your mother, and when you want to distract your mother from the discouraging soulness, I will tell you what I used to do. To take her for a long walk in the quiet country, gathering wild flowers here and there, resting under the shade of trees, between the harmony of the vivid stream and the gentle tranquility of the mothernature, and I am sure that she will enjoy this very much, as you surely would be happy for it. But remember always, Dante, in the play of happiness, don't you use all for yourself only, but down yourself just one step, at your side and help the weak ones that cry for help, help the prosecuted and the victim, because that are your better friends;

they are the comrades that fight and fall as your father and Bartolo fought and fell yesterday for the conquest of the joy of freedom for all and the poor workers. In this struggle of life you will find more love and you will be loved.

I am sure that from what your mother told me about what you said during these last terrible days when I was lying in the iniquitous death house — that description gave me happiness because it showed you will be the beloved boy I had always dreamed.

Therefore whatever should happen tomorrow, nobody knows, but if they should kill us, you must not forget to look at your friends and comrades with the smiling gaze of gratitude as you look at your beloved ones, because they love you as they love every one of the fallen persecuted comrades. I tell you, your father that is all the life to you, your father that loved you and saw them, and knows their noble faith (that is mine) their supreme sacrifice that they are still doing for our freedom, for I have fought with them, and they are the ones that still hold the last of our hope that today they can still save us from electrocution, it is the struggle and fight between the rich and the poor for safety and freedom, Son, which you will understand in the future of your years to come, of this unrest and struggle of life's death.

Much I thought of you when I was lying in the death house — the singing, the kind tender voices of the children from the playground, where there was all the life and the joy of liberty — just one step from the wall which contains the buried agony of three buried souls. It would remind me so often of you and your sister Ines, and I wish I could see you every moment. But I feel better that you did not come to the death house so that you could not see the horrible picture of three lying in agony waiting to be electrocuted, because I do not know what effect it would have on your young age. But then, in another way if you were not so sensitive it would be very useful to you tomorrow when you could use this horrible memory to holdup to the world the shame of the country in this cruel persecution and unjust death. Yes, Dante, they can crucify our bodies today as they are doing, but they cannot destroy our ideas, that will remain for the youth of the future to come.

Dante, when I said three human lives buried, I meant to say that with us there is another young man by the name of Celestino Maderios that is to be electrocuted at the same time with us. He has been twice before in that horrible death house, that should be destroyed with the hammers of real progress — that horrible house that will shame forever the future of the citizens of Massachusetts. They should destroy that house and put up a factory or school, to teach many of the hundreds of the poor orphan boys of the world.

Dante, I say once more to love and be nearest to your mother and the beloved ones in these sad days, and I am sure that with your brave heart and kind goodness they will feel less discomfort. And you will also not forget to love me a little for I do — O, Sonny! thinking so much and so often of you.

Best fraternal greetings to all the beloved ones, love and kisses to your little Ines and mother. Most hearty affectionate embrace.

Your Father and Companion

P.S. Bartolo send you the most affectionate greetings. I hope that your mother will help you to understand this letter because I could have written much better and more simple, if I was feeling good. But I am so weak.

Sacco and Vanzetti to the
Sacco-Vanzetti Defense Committee

August 21, 1927
From the Death House of Massachusetts State Prison

Dear Friends and Comrades of the Sacco-Vanzetti Defense Committee,
After tomorrow midnight, we will be executed, save a new stay of execution by either the United States Supreme Court or by Governor Alvan T. Fuller.

We have no hope. This morning, our brave defender and friend Michael Angelo Musmanno was here from his return from Washington, and told us he would come back this afternoon if he would have time for it. Also Rosa and Luigi were here this morning and they too, promised us to return this afternoon. But now it is 5:30 p.m. and no one returned yet. This tells us there is no good news for us, for, if so, some of you would have hurried to bring them to us. It almost tells us all your efforts have failed and that you are spending these remaining few hours in desperate and hopeless efforts to evitate our execution. In a word, we feel lost! Therefore, we decided to write this letter to you to express our gratitude and admiration for all what you have done in our defense during these seven years, four months and eleven days of struggle.

That we have lost and have to die does not diminish our appreciation and gratitude for your great solidarity with us and our families.

Friends and comrades, now that the tragedy of this trial is at an end, be all as one heart. Only two of us will die. Our ideal, you our comrades, will live by millions; we have won, but not vanquished. Just treasure our suffering, our sorrow, our mistakes, our defeats, our passion for future battles and for the great emancipation.

Be all as of one heart in this blackest hour of our tragedy. And have heart.

Salute for us all the friends and comrades of the earth.

We embrace you all, and bid you all our extreme good-bye with our hearts filled with love and affection. Now and ever, long life to you all, long life to Liberty.

Yours in Life and Death,
Bartolomeo Vanzetti
Nicola Sacco

part two:

The Cause Célèbre

Edna St. Vincent Millay
Justice Denied in Massachusetts (1927)
(an excerpt)

Let us go home, and sit in the sitting-room.
Not in our day
Shall the cloud go over and the sun rise as before,
Beneficent upon us
Out of the glittering bay,
And the warm winds be blown inward from the sea
Moving the blades of corn
With a peaceful sound.
Forlorn, forlorn,
Stands the blue hay-rack by the empty mow.
And the petals drop to the ground,
Leaving the tree unfruited.
The sun that warmed our stooping backs and
withered the weed uprooted —
We shall not feel it again.
We shall die in darkness, and be buried in the rain.

John Dos Passos

Novelist John Dos Passos was active on the Defense Committee, and wrote Sacco and Vanzetti's formal plea to be presented in court.

Save Sacco and Vanzetti
The Defense Committee's Plea

Where are Sacco and Vanzetti in all this? A broken man in Charlestown, a broken man in a gray bird cage in Dedham, struggling to keep some shreds of human dignity in face of the Chair? Not at all.

Circumstances sometimes force men into situations so dramatic, thrust their puny frames so far into the burning bright searchlights of history, that they or their shadows on men's minds become enormous symbols. Sacco and Vanzetti are all the immigrants who have built this nation's industries with their sweat and their blood and have gotten for it nothing but the smallest wage it was possible to give them and a helot's position under the boot heels of the Arrow Collar social order. They are all the wops, hunkies, bohunks, factory fodder that hunger drives into the American mills through the painful sieve of Ellis Island. They are the dreams of a saner social order of those who can't stand the law of dawg eat dawg. This tiny courtroom is a focus of the turmoil of an age of tradition, the center of eyes all over the world. Sacco and Vanzetti throw enormous shadows on the court house walls.

[Defense Lawyer] William G. Thompson feels all this dimly when, the last affidavit read, he pauses to begin his argument. But mostly he feels that as a citizen it is his duty to protect the laws and liberties of his state, and as a man to try to save two innocent men from being murdered by a machine set going in a moment of hatred and panic. He is a broad shouldered man with steely white hair and a broad forehead and broad cheekbones. He doesn't mince words. He feels things intensely. The case is no legal game of chess for him.

"I rest my case on these affidavits, on the other five propositions that I have argued, but if they all fail, and I cannot see how they can, I rest my case on that rock alone, on the sixth proposition in my brief — innocent or guilty, right or wrong, foolish or wise men — these men ought not now to be sentenced to death for this crime so long as they have the right to say, 'The government of this great country put spies in my cell, planned to put spies in my wife's house, they put spies on my friends, took money that they were collecting to defend me, put it in their own pocket and joked about it and said they don't believe I am guilty but will help convict me, because they could not get enough evidence to deport me under the laws of congress, and were willing as one of them continually said to adopt the method of killing me for murder as one way to get rid of me.'"...

Then the dry, crackling, careful voice of Judge Thayer and the hearing is adjourned.

Hear ye, hear ye, hear ye, all who have had business before the honorable, the justice of the superior court of the southeastern district of Massachusetts, will now disperse. The court is adjourned without day.

God Save the Commonwealth of Massachusetts.

The court refused to grant a new trial. The Court has decided that Sacco and Vanzetti must die.

God Save the Commonwealth of Massachusetts...

How is all this possible? Why were these men ever convicted in the first place? From the calm of the year of our Lord 1926 it's pretty hard to remember the delirious year 1920...

The faces of men who have been a long time in jail have a peculiar frozen look under the eyes. The face of a man who has been a long time in jail never loses that tightness under the eyes. Sacco has been six years in the county jail, always waiting, waiting for trial, waiting for new evidence, waiting for motions to be argued, waiting for sentence, waiting, waiting, waiting. The Dedham Jail is a handsome structure, set among lawns, screened by trees that wave new green leaves against the robins-egg sky of June. In the warden's office you can see your face in the light brown varnish, you could eat eggs off the floor it is so clean. Inside the main reception hall it is airy, full of sunlight. The bars are bright with reflected spring greens, a fresh pea-green light is over everything. Through the bars you can see the waving trees and the June clouds roaming the sky like cattle in an unfenced pasture. It's a preposterous complicated canary cage. Why aren't the birds singing in this green aviary? The warden politely shows you a seat and as you wait you notice a smell, not green and airy this smell, a jaded heavy greasy smell of slum, like the smell of army slum, but heavier, more hopeless.

Across the hall an old man is sitting in a chair, a heavy pear-shaped man, his hands limp at his sides, his eyes are closed, his sagged face is like a bundle of wet newspapers. The warden and two men in black stand over him, looking down at him help-lessly.

At last Sacco has come out of his cell and sits beside me. Two men sitting side by side on a bench in a green bird cage. When he feels like it one of them will get up and walk out, walk out into the sunny June day. The other will go back to his cell to wait. He looks younger than I had expected. His face has a waxy transparency, like the face of a man who's been sick in bed for a long time; when he laughs his cheeks flush a little. At length we manage both of us to laugh. It's such a preposterous position for a man to be in, like a man who doesn't know the game trying to play chess blindfolded. The real world has gone. We have no more grasp of our world of rain and streets and trolley cars and cucumber vines and girls and garden plots. This is a world of phrases: prosecution, defense, evidence, motion, irrelevant, incompetent and immaterial. For six years this man has lived in the law, tied tighter and tighter in the sticky filaments of law-words like a fly in a spider web. And the wrong set of words means the Chair. All the moves in the game are made for him, all he can do is sit helpless and wait, fastening his hopes on one set of phrases after another. In all these law books, in all this terminology of clerks of the court and counsel for the defense there is one move that will save him, out of a million that will mean death. If only they make the right move, use the right words. But by this time the nagging torment of hope has almost stopped, not even the thought of his wife and children out there in the world, unreachable, can torture him now. He is numb now, can laugh and look quizzically at the ponderous machine that has caught and mangled him. Now it hardly matters to him if they do manage to pull him out from between the cogs, and the wrong set of words means the Chair...

Going to the State Prison at Charlestown is more like going to Barnum and Baileys. There's a great scurry of guards, groups of people waiting outside; inside a brass band is playing "Home Sweet Home." When at length you get let into the Big Show, you find a great many things happening at once. There are rows of chairs where pairs of people sit talking. Each pair is made up of a free man and a convict. In three directions there are gray bars and tiers of cells. The band inside plays bangingly "If Auld Acquaintance Be Forgot." A short broad-shouldered man is sitting quiet through all the uproar, smiling a little under his big drooping mustache. He has a domed, pale forehead and black eyes surrounded by many little wrinkles. The serene modeling of his cheekbones and hollow cheeks makes you forget the prison look under his eyes.

This is Vanzetti.

And for the last six years, three hundred and sixty-five days a year, yesterday, today, tomorrow, Sacco and Vanzetti wake up on their prison pallets, eat prison food, have an hour of exercise and conversation a day, sit in their cells puzzling about this technicality and that technicality, pinning their hopes to their alibis, to the expert testimony about the character of the barrel of Sacco's gun, to Madeiros' confession and Weeks' corroboration, to action before the Supreme Court of the United States, and day by day the props are dashed from under their feet and they feel themselves being inexorably pushed toward the Chair by the blind hatred of thousands of well-meaning citizens, by the superhuman, involved, stealthy, soulless mechanism of the law...

What is going to be done if the Supreme Judicial Court continues to refuse Sacco and Vanzetti a new trial? Are Sacco and Vanzetti going to burn in the Chair?

The conscience of the people of Massachusetts must be awakened. Working people, underdogs, Reds, know instinctively what is going on. The same thing has happened before. But the average law-admiring, authority-respecting citizen does not know. For the first time, since Judge Thayer's last denial of motions for a new trial, there has been a certain awakening among the influential part of the community, the part of the community respected by the press and the bench and the pulpit. Always there have been notable exceptions, but up to now these good citizens have had no suspicion that anything but justice was being meted out by the courts. Goaded by the *New York World* editorials, Chief Counsel Thompson's eloquence, by the *Boston Herald's* courageous change of front, they are getting uneasy. It remains to be seen what will come of this uneasiness. The *Boston Herald* suggests an impartial commission to review the whole case. All that is needed is that the facts of the case be generally known.

Everyone must work to that end, no matter what happens, that the facts of the case may be known so that no one can plead ignorance, so that if these men are killed, everyone in the state, everyone in the country will have the guilt on them. So that no one can say "I would have protested but I didn't know what was being done."

Tell your friends, write to your congressmen, to the political bosses of your district, to the newspapers. Demand the truth about Sacco and Vanzetti. Call meetings, try to line up trade unions, organizations, clubs, put up posters. Demand the truth about Sacco and Vanzetti.

If the truth had been told they would be free men today.

If the truth is not told they will burn in the Chair in Charlestown Jail. If they die what little faith many millions of men have in the chance of justice in this country will die with them.

Source: John Dos Passos, *Save Sacco and Vanzetti, Facing the Chair: Story of the Americanization of Two Foreignborn Working Men* (Boston: Sacco and Vanzetti Defense Committee, 1927)

Elizabeth Glendower Evans

Suffragist Elizabeth Glendower Evans wrote regularly to both men during their imprisonment. This article was first published in the New Republic, *June 8, 1921.*

Foreigners

Bartolomeo Vanzetti, on trial with another Italian named Sacco, for a payroll robbery and murder which occurred in Braintree a year ago, is serving a 15 year sentence in State Prison for an earlier attempt at a payroll holdup at Bridgewater, of which he was found guilty last July. There are circumstances connected with this arrest and trial, which suggest a grave miscarriage of justice, and if he is acquitted at his impending trial, there will be a motion to secure a new trial for the Bridgewater affair.

Vanzetti is a determined-looking man, big and powerful, and somewhat stern of expression. His features are shapely, and he has a very winning smile. His command of English is limited, but he is making use of his time in prison to study English and spelling and "arithmatics," as he quaintly pronounced the word. He made no effort to converse, but responded with simplicity to my various leads. When I asked him about his home in Italy, if he thought of it often, his face lighted. "Oh, I think of it all the time. I can see my father's house and the pear tree near the door. I can see it all as if it were here." I had heard that he was esteemed by his fellows as a thinker, and as one who has his ideals much at heart. And of this, his conversation gave abundant proof.

Since I saw him in prison, I have read a little article of his which had been published in an Italian newspaper, to which he has been a frequent contributor. In this article, which is entitled "Glimpses of My Intellectual Life," he tells of how in his youth he read St. Augustine and Dante's *Divine Comedy*. As a result of such reading, Vanzetti wrote: "Humanity and Equality of Rights began to afflict my heart… Later I realized that the worst evil that torments Humanity is Ignorance, and Degeneration of Natural Susceptibility. My religion no longer needed an altar or temple or formal prayers; God, to me, was the Universe, of which I felt to be an insignificant particle, the spiritual spoils of every human attribute."

At his trial in Plymouth, Vanzetti was asked by the prosecuting officer, "Are you an anarchist?", and his answer suggested his life story: "Well, I don't know what you call it. I am a little different… I like things a little different…" Low wages and long hours and unemployment and rough toil have been his portion in this land where he had sought to realize his boyhood dreams. No wonder he "likes things a little different."

The transcript of the evidence in the preliminary hearing upon which Sacco and Vanzetti were arraigned, and the transcript of Vanzetti's trial, are a matter of record of which the counsel for the defense secured a copy for us in preparing for the pending trial. (Incidentally, this made a drain upon the defense fund of some $700 to obtain evidence which it would seem the government should have supplied gratuitously.) A more astonishing document surely never met mortal eyes.

No evidence is given showing why either Sacco or Vanzetti should have been held for the Braintree crime. If further evidence exists, the accused were given no chance to meet it. While the only evidence connecting Vanzetti with the Bridgewater affair which afforded ground for more than a surmise was that of persons who had witnessed the holdup and who claimed to recognize one of the men who had done the shooting — a man, be it remembered, they had never seen before, and of whom they got but a momentary glance upon an occasion of intense excitement. An interval of four months had elapsed between this occasion and the first attempt at identification, and between two and three more months elapsed before the attempted identification at the trial. All but two of the witnesses, while they were fairly positive in their identification, admitted that there was room for doubt. "I think he is the man"; "I feel so, but I may be mistaken."

Two witnesses, to be sure, were positive in their identification. One of these, about 15 minutes before the holdup occurred, had noticed a covered motor with the windshield up, standing some distance up the street, and she claimed to have particularly observed the man at the wheel, whom she was sure was Vanzetti. But this witness was equally sure that she had seen the shooting, had seen the fire from the gun. And this she certainly did not see, as cross-examination developed the fact that a two-story building obstructed the line of vision between the scene of action and her point of observation from a window in the railroad station. Another witness, a school boy, who was equally positive that the man who fired the gun was the man before him in the dock, admitted that he got but a "fleeting glance," and the only description he could give was that "by the way he ran, I could tell he was a foreigner."

Not one witness who described the gunman made note of the unusually big mustache which is the striking feature of Vanzetti's physiognomy. The mustache of the bandit is variously described as "short," "croppy," "trimmed," "neither big nor small," "not a Charlie Chaplin mustache," "a mustache that had been cropped off at the end — not long and flowing." When I visited Vanzetti in prison, I could discern not one single point in his appearance which had been suggested by any of the identifications.

To meet testimony which it is difficult to regard as serious, the defense produced a long line of witnesses who swore that Vanzetti had been on his accustomed fish route at Plymouth from early morning into the afternoon of the day that the holdup occurred in a city 28 miles distant. The landlady who had roused him at six o'clock when a neighbor called with an order for fish, the man who keeps a little shop nearby, the boy who helped peddle fish from the cart and thereby earned his Christmas money, nine different housewives who had bought their day-before-Christmas dinner from Vanzetti, all offered testimony which had in it no element of discrepancy.

Such was the important evidence both for the prosecution and for the defense, as recorded in the official transcript of Vanzetti's trial. And when in the face of this evidence the jury brought in a verdict of "guilty," one had a confused sense of non sequitur, such as one feels when a prestidigitator produces a rabbit out of a hat.

That "twelve good men and true" should have brought in so amazing a verdict, and that it should be followed by a sentence of 15 years in State Prison, is almost incredible. Other factors must have been present (so it will be argued) which are not here set down. And to some degree this is true. For, however intangible and discrepant the evidence presented by the prosecution was in most respects, upon one point all were agreed: the man who committed the crime was "some kind of foreigner"; he was "dark-complexioned"; he was "swarthy — like an Italian"; "he was a foreigner of some kind"; he could even be recognized as a foreigner by "the way he ran"! Similarly, there was the fact that "foreigners" were the only witnesses produced on behalf of the accused. Is this the reason that Vanzetti is serving a term of 15 years in prison?

These things happened in the early months of 1920 when the

anti-alien hysteria which had been gathering head since the war was at its climax. Aliens were presumably "Reds" and "Reds" were outside the pale of the law. Witnesses and court officials and jurymen of Cape Cod were presumably not immune from this mob psychology. Is this suggestion resented? In the days of the witchcraft delusions, did not the godly folk of New England see a witch in every old woman, and believe with the most perfect conviction that they beheld them riding on broomsticks across the sky?

Meanwhile working-class Italians, in these days of bitter unemployment, are taxing themselves for the defense fund with a generosity beyond the understanding of those who belong to the more protected class. One man had quit a job at which he earned $43 a week, and puts in his whole time helping on the case. Another mortgaged his little home for $1,500, and gave the money to the defense fund without hope of ever getting back one cent. Others drew out every dollar from the savings bank. Shall such as these carry the whole burden.

Eugene V. Debs

Socialist leader Eugene V. Debs supported the two anarchists throughout their imprisonment and made this statement in October 1926.

Statement

The Supreme Court of Massachusetts has spoken at last and Bartolomeo Vanzetti and Nicola Sacco, two of the bravest and best scouts that ever served the labor movement, must go to the electric chair. The decision of this capitalistic judicial tribunal is not surprising. It accords perfectly with the tragical farce and the farcical tragedy of the entire trial of these two absolutely innocent and shamefully persecuted working men.

Now is the time for all labor to be aroused and to rally as one vast hope to vindicate its assailed honor, to assert its self-respect, and to issue its demand that in spite of the capitalist-controlled courts of Massachusetts, honest and innocent working men whose only crime is their innocence of crime and their loyalty to labor, shall not be murdered by the official hirings of the corporate powers that rule and tyrannize over the state.

James P. Cannon

*James P. Cannon was a founder of the
Communist Party USA and active in the labor movement.
He made this speech at the Sacco-Vanzetti Mass Meeting
in Chicago on May 13, 1927, and it was published
in the June 1927 edition of the* Labor Defender.

A Speech for Sacco and Vanzetti

The Sacco-Vanzetti case has been a part of American labor history in the making. It is seven years now since Sacco and Vanzetti have been in the shadow of the electric chair. I do not believe that history knows of a similar case. I do not believe that we could find anywhere a case of such prolonged torture as the holding of the sentence of death over the heads of men for seven years. At the end of that time we come together for a meeting and do not know yet whether that sentence is to be executed or not.

The cause of Sacco and Vanzetti demands of us, of the entire labor movement, militant, unhesitating and united support. We may have different opinions on many problems; but there is one thing we have become sure of in these seven years in which we have said our word for Sacco and Vanzetti. We have become absolutely convinced that the case of Sacco and Vanzetti, the case of these two Italian workers in Massachusetts, is not the case of two holdup men or bandits. We have become convinced that it is the working class against the capitalists. We have become convinced that Sacco and Vanzetti are not only innocent of this specific crime which they are charged with, but that they are innocent of any crime except that of being rebels against capitalist exploitation of the masses.

Their case has gone so far that we do not need to discuss it any longer from a legal standpoint. But for those who are interested, it has been set forth by Mr. Holly. And we can say for others, that recently a book was published by Professor Felix Frankfurter in which he comes to the conclusion that there is no legal case against Sacco and Vanzetti.

But the case of Sacco and Vanzetti has a far bigger significance than any legal procedure. Sacco and Vanzetti began in this case as two employees, obscure fighters of the working class. But they have grown in these years, until their personalities have made their impression not only in Massachusetts, not only in the United States, but all over Europe and America.

Sacco and Vanzetti have grown as the great symbols of the whole labor movement. They stand for the upward struggle against oppression and exploitation, for that fearless defiance of the enemies of labor with which the best representatives of the working class are instinct.

Everyone today knows why the Bourbons of Massachusetts arrested, imprisoned and tried Sacco and Vanzetti. Had they not been scrupulously loyal to the cause of the working class, they would not now be faced with the grim march to the death chair. Had they remained silent while their brothers and comrades around them suffered persecution and oppression, had they not made the ideal of the liberation of the working class their own ideal, there would not today be a Sacco-Vanzetti case. Had they, in court, begged for mercy and renounced their cause and their past, they would have been freed to achieve obloquy.

But they did none of this. Despite the hundreds of interminable nights and days of imprisonment, with the ghastly thought of execution constantly in their minds, they have remained as simply true to the workers' cause as they were before this infamous frame-up was conceived in the minds of the Massachusetts reaction. Yes, their persecution has even steeled their convictions, and has already bound them inseparably with the history of the American labor movement.

After seven years they came to court for sentence. I wish every worker in America could read the speech that Vanzetti made there. After seven years of torture, with the death sentence hanging over him, this man stood up in court, not as one guilty, not as one afraid. He turned to the judge on the bench and said to him:

"You are the one that is afraid. You are the one that is shrinking with fear, because you are the one that is guilty of attempt to murder."

Vanzetti called his witnesses there, and not merely legal witnesses. He marshaled before Judge Thayer's attention the thousands who have decided to hold mass meetings such as ours; and public men of our period like Anatole France, Maxim Gorki, Bernard Shaw, Henri Barbusse, Albert Einstein. He pointed to the many millions who have protested against the frame-up.

He turned to Eugene Victor Debs and other men in America. Let us not forget that we should measure guilt and innocence not by formal evidence in court alone, but by higher values than that. Let us not forget that the last thing that Eugene Debs wrote publicly was an appeal to the workers of America for Sacco and Vanzetti, an appeal whose stirring language aroused with renewed vigor the protest of hundreds of thousands in this country, and brought again the million-voiced demand for life and freedom for these two valiant fighters, and condemnation of their persecutors.

It is hard to speak with restraint. I, like Comrade Chaplin, also had the honor of talking with Vanzetti. Everyone that has seen and talked with him comes away with the feeling that he has stood in the presence of one of the greatest spirits of our time.

It is hard to speak with restraint when one is pressed by the thought that the vengeful executioners of Massachusetts are consummating their hideous plan to press the switch that will forever remove from our ranks the persons of these two men who we feel are so much a part of labor and its cause. Our impassioned determination to mobilize all of our strength and power to rescue Sacco and Vanzetti from their blood-lusting jailers must be communicated throughout the land, if we are to save them from the fate that has been prepared for them.

While I agree with the statements of Fitzpatrick that our meeting should dissociate itself from irresponsible people, let us not forget the year 1915 when Joe Hill was killed in Utah. We must remember that when the wave of working-class protest began to rise in protection of Joe Hill, gangs of detectives began to fake threatening letters. After the heart of Joe Hill had been pierced by the bullets of the death squad, it was exposed that frame-up letters had been used. This must be a lesson for us and for those who are the friends of Sacco and Vanzetti.

There is no need to threaten the governor or anyone else because the protection of Sacco and Vanzetti is far stronger than any personal act. The protection of Sacco and Vanzetti is the job of the working class of the world, which is knocking on the door, not with the hands of irresponsible individuals, but with the titanic fist of the workers of the wide world, because they believe in the innocence of Sacco and Vanzetti. We say to you, our friends and our chairman, before they turn on the switch, that the real aim is not only to burn Sacco and Vanzetti in the electric chair but to burn the labor movement in America.

If the workers of America and the workers of the world are

determined enough and encouraged enough, we can yet save Sacco and Vanzetti. And it is in that spirit that we meet here tonight. We do not meet here to resign ourselves to their fate. We meet as another stage in the fight for Sacco and Vanzetti. We believe that the workers assembled here will go back to their organizations and their jobs and raise again the battle cry for Sacco and Vanzetti.

Anatole France

French writer and Nobel Prize laureate Anatole France wrote the following for the November 1921 edition of The Nation.

To the People of America

La Bêchellerie, October 31

People of the United States of America, hearken to the words of an old man of the Old World, who is not alien to you, for he is a fellow-citizen of all men.

In one of your states, two men, Sacco and Vanzetti, have been condemned for a crime of opinion.

It is horrible to think that human beings should pay with their lives for the exercise of that most sacred right, the right which we ought all to defend, to whatever party we may belong.

Do not let this most iniquitous of sentences be carried out.

The death of Sacco and of Vanzetti would make martyrs of them, and would cover all of you with shame.

You are a great people; you ought to be a just people. There are among you plenty of men of intelligence, men who think. It is to them that I prefer to appeal. I say to them: Fear to make martyrs. It is the unpardonable crime, which nothing can obliterate and which weighs upon generation after generation.

Save Sacco and Vanzetti.

Save them for your honor, for the honor of your children and of all the generations yet unborn.

Bruce Bliven

Journalist Bruce Bliven joined the New Republic in 1923, writing regularly on the case, including this article from June 29, 1927.

Boston's Civil War

Boston has been profoundly stirred by the Sacco-Vanzetti case. To an amazing degree, the city is at present absorbed in, and obsessed by this affair of two Italian radicals, a fish-peddler and a factory hand, who have been sentenced to die in the electric chair during the week of July 10, for a murder which they almost certainly did not commit, and after a trial which, beyond any shadow of a reasonable doubt, was unfair.

The subject has occasioned a controversy of extraordinary bitterness; for a parallel, one must go back to the Dreyfus case, which this one, indeed, resembles. In American history, perhaps nothing since the slavery dispute before the Civil War has created such violent differences of opinion among persons who would ordinarily think alike. In two Boston clubs, to my knowledge, and probably in others, members have been forbidden by formal rule to talk about the "S-V affair." In these organizations, opinion is against the two Italians by at least 20 to one; but even so, the arguments have been so acrimonious that it was felt necessary to prohibit them. Families have been divided; business partners disagree, and always with passion. No one seems capable of being lukewarm about the affair. Which, I submit, is as it should be. For it is a serious business, this putting to death of two men who, almost beyond doubt, are innocent, merely because, at a time of great popular hysteria, they happen to become living symbols of opposition to "God, country and property."

On the whole, the upper strata of the social layer-cake in Boston support Judge Thayer, and demand that Sacco and Vanzetti shall be put to death without more ado. It is impossible, of course, to offer any statistics in support of this statement. Certainly there are many honorable exceptions, individuals who have come forward and put themselves on record — sometimes at great sacrifice — as believing that the Italians did not have a fair trial. I have been told by one observer that the leaders of the bar, for example, are divided about equally; but all the other evidence I have been able to gather makes me believe, on the contrary, that those who do not want the sentence disturbed constitute an overwhelming majority. This is probably also true among the lower middle class. Its members are likely to take their opinions, in a matter of this sort, from their employers or from some industrial or financial leader whose views they may chance to see published in the newspapers.

Among the workers, opinion in general favors Sacco and Vanzetti, though it is not unanimous. All the unions affiliated with the American Federation of Labor are solidly behind the defense, and have furnished invaluable aid, financial and moral. The Italians are also supporting their fellow countrymen, and this is true even of most of the Boston Fascisti, who let consanguinity override their political disagreement with the anarchists. Were it not for the faithful support of a small group of Italians, most of them radicals, the chances are that Sacco and Vanzetti would long ago have gone to the chair. It was this group which organized the defense, and contributed the funds to carry on the fight, long before most of the American liberals knew anything about the case.

While, as I say, I cannot prove that the sentiment against Sacco and Vanzetti controls a numerical majority of the upper class, that it is tremendously powerful I can show by several pieces of evidence.

There is, *item,* the fact that the Harvard Law School drive for funds has been handicapped because of activities of some of its faculty in seeking to have the trial reviewed. The handicap, I am glad to say, has not been fatal; but it has been serious. (The Yale Law School, whose faculty took a similar position, has also been subjected to what can only be described as attempted terrorization, and this terrorization has come from some of those very leaders of the bar who should be most jealous to safeguard the processes of justice from any taint of unfairness.)

There is, *item*, the overwhelming demand that "outsiders" shall not interfere in the case, a demand which comes exclusively from those who support Judge Thayer. On the day that I arrived in Boston, for example, Mr. John C. Hull, speaker of [the] Massachusetts House of Representatives, in an address at a banquet of "best citizens," voiced what he said is the state's demand of all outsiders: "We would respectfully ask you to mind your own business." Whereupon, according to the newspaper reports, the 750 persons present leaped to their feet and burst into a storm of applause. Shortly before this, the Braintree Board of Trade wrote to Governor Fuller: "We are opposed to outside agencies and influences interfering with the liberties and institutions we enjoy." Numerous letters have appeared in the press similar to that of Mr. Alfred S. Hewins, who observed in the *Evening Transcript*: "To what a pass have we come in the commonwealth if we cannot say who is guilty or who is not guilty of breaking the laws."

There is, *item*, the fact that most Boston bookstores do not display the volume by Professor Felix Frankfurter, of Harvard Law School, which tells the story of the case. They have it in stock, and, if you ask for it, they will produce a copy for you, but the stores I visited did not have it anywhere in sight, and I am advised that this is true of most of the others. Yet, if public interest were the criterion, these stores should display nothing else.

There is, *item*, the refusal to permit children in schools to discuss the case. On the same day that Mr. Hull made his speech, Miss Sarah McGrory, a teacher in the Brockton High School, achieved a temporary fame by declining to allow those sheltered darlings, her pupils, to hear a debate on the subject. This was on the ground, so far as I can gather, that the whole matter is "low." The headmaster, one Lewis E. Rye, supported her action.

There is, *item*, the punishment the community inflicts, when it can, on individuals who become identified with the unpopular view. This is a matter which cannot be discussed adequately within the limits of a brief article; and it deals with personal experiences which are not appropriate for public recital. But a sufficient number of incidents have been related to me, in confidence, amply to warrant the statement that, where it is possible to penalize an individual for taking the "wrong side," the screws have been put on.

Among the sufferers are not only attorneys and other practitioners of the professions, dependent on the good will of clients, but some newspaper men whose views are at variance with those of their journals. One case of this sort will suffice to point out to my readers a situation which, after all, is far from unique in American journalism. An important Boston paper assigned one of its men to make a careful investigation of the whole case. This he did, and came out convinced not only that the two men did not have a fair trial, but that they are completely innocent. He communicated his findings to his paper — and was promptly assigned to other tasks. Since then, everything written for that journal on the Sacco-Vanzetti case has been the work of other men, uncorrupted by any intimate knowledge of the facts, and has been unfavorable to the Italians.

There is, *item*, the muzzling of the press in general, a matter so important that it warrants discussion in some detail. I am not so naive as to suggest that somebody higher up has actually told any editor to oppose a review of the case. Anything so crude as that almost never happens. What has taken place is that the editors, sensing the drift of community opinion, have (perhaps in some cases unconsciously) drifted with it.

I have read, in the past few days, every line printed in every Boston newspaper on this case since it became a burning issue with the news of the Supreme Court's final decision; and all important items for some years before that. It is an interesting, if somewhat melancholy, experience to note the progressive timidity in the tone of the editorial comment of most papers, as public feeling has grown more bitter. Almost equally striking is the decrease in quantity. Throughout the case, all the papers have printed the day-to-day facts, with, so far as I could judge, accuracy and fairness, although, repeatedly, items which seem to me of high news value have been buried on a remote inside page, have been written with utmost brevity, and printed under headlines so quiet (for Boston) as to be almost speechless. It is with editorial discussion, however, that I am here concerned. Of that, there has been amazingly little, in view of the overwhelming interest in the case. News articles have outnumbered editorials 50 to one.

When the famous affidavits were made public, charging Judge Thayer with prejudice, most of the papers refrained from any comment whatever. The appointment of Dr. Lowell, Dr. Stratton and Judge Grant as an advisory board was greeted with timorous approval by one or two papers and with silence by the rest — except the *Evening Transcript*. That paper, which has steadily fought against Sacco and Vanzetti, remarked that "we can see neither reason nor justification for the appointment by Governor Fuller of an advisory commission."

One of the leading papers of Boston, which, in the earlier days of the case, had spoken out vigorously in favor of a review of the evidence, during these critical months has centered its editorial efforts on three things: (a) pointing out to its readers the desirability of reading Professor Frankfurter's article in the *Atlantic Monthly* for March; (b) urging them to peruse the subsequent debate between Professor Frankfurter and Dean John H. Wigmore of Northwestern Law School in the *Evening Transcript*; (c) criticizing a cartoon which appeared in *Life*.

Among the best-edited of the Boston papers is the *Herald*, which has done a noteworthy service in opening its correspondence columns to letters giving every possible view of this famous case. The *Herald*, as our readers may remember, last year published a ringing editorial entitled "We Submit — ," giving an admirable summary of the evidence which showed the desirability of a new trial. This editorial was published anonymously, with the full weight of the paper behind it. It won for its author, Mr. F. Lauriston Bullard, the Pulitzer Prize for 1926. When this fact was announced a few weeks ago, the *Herald* celebrated the occasion with these extraordinary words:

"When a Pulitzer Prize last came our way three years ago... we felt disposed to shout, 'All hands up; three cheers.' This time the subject is so solemn, involving not only human lives but the larger questions of law enforcement and exact justice, that we refrain from any note of jubilation and merely express our hope that the longer testimony of the years will afford corroboration of the author's view..."

This incident is not mentioned with any purpose of singling the *Herald* out for adverse criticism. That paper has certainly behaved better than most Boston journals. I mention it merely to indicate the unusual character of the social strain which the community is feeling.

If you think of the fine traditions of Boston, of the giants this city bred in other days, it is a saddening experience to visit it now, and see so many sons of the Puritans who are false to their heritage. And yet there are some things to put into the other side of the scale as well. One remembers the dozens of men, the intellectual leaders of the community — college professors, church dignitaries, lawyers, businessmen — who have come forward and given their time, their money, the weight of their names, at no small sacrifice, in order to prevent, if they can, the unjust death of two men with whom they are in utter disagreement. One thinks of the Italians (and Americans) of the Sacco-Vanzetti Defense Committee, working long years in their little dingy third-floor room, collecting, penny by penny, huge sums which have been disbursed in the terribly expensive processes of the law. Of men like Professor Frankfurter and Dean Pound of Harvard Law School, fighting steadfastly and skillfully for the honor of their profession against fellow practitioners who would defame its temple. Of William G. Thompson, silver-haired, rugged Yankee, a man as far as possible in philosophy from Sacco and Vanzetti, who has devoted years to a desperate struggle which sneering bystanders pronounce quixotic, that Justice shall prevail. And so one looks again at Boston, with clearer eyes, and perceives that the old Americanism is not dead, after all. Through the murky smoke of commerce, the spark may still be seen, alive on the altar.

The Nation

The Nation, *August 1927.*

World Opinion on Sacco and Vanzetti

No more striking evidence of the international character of the Sacco and Vanzetti case can be presented than appears in the editorial columns of foreign newspapers and periodicals. Conservative and liberal journals alike unite in featuring the news of the case. By actual count 12 leading Paris newspapers on August 5 devoted four times as much space to the Sacco and Vanzetti case as to the break up of the Geneva Conference. And the editorials show a remarkable unanimity of opinion: that something is radically wrong with U.S. justice. We quote below the more significant statements.

The London *Times* (August 11):

> A postponement once again must intensify feeling widely prevalent all over the world, whether the condemned men are guilty or not, that the prolonged suffering which they have undergone during seven years under the sentence of death makes them fit objects of pity.

The London *Spectator*, a conservative weekly (August 13), waiving the question of the men's guilt, hopes that they will be reprieved:

Because that would be best, not only for peace but for the credit of the United States. Certain facts make us feel that justice in the strict sense of the word would be truly served either by the release of the prisoners or by a further term of imprisonment, the greater part of which might be taken as having been already satisfied by the six years under which the prisoners have lain under sentence of death.

The London *Outlook,* mildly liberal, (August 13) comments:

In themselves Sacco and Vanzetti are obscure and without any political importance. But they have become a symbol to millions of people throughout the world as victims of the "capitalist" system of justice, which has one law for the poor and another for the rich. The case has intensified class antagonism throughout the world. It is difficult to judge the case on its merits, but there is no question that there is something radically wrong with American administration of law.

The London *Daily News* (August 11):

No one whatever ought to be treated as these men, whatever they have done. Surely there must be someone in America, President Coolidge or another, capable of quietly making effective this obvious truth.

The question now is whether that is enough or whether patriotic Americans can suffer longer a criminal system so rigid and stiff in its pedantry and in its tender mercies worse than the excesses of barbarism.

The Liverpool *Post* in an editorial said (August 9):

The original trial from start to finish was a travesty of judicial procedure. It was so understood among most of the European peoples and we can readily believe it was so understood in America as a whole.

The Paris *Journal des Débats* (conservative) August 4:

> The decision of Governor Fuller has caused profound sur-
> prise and real regret in France. We still believe that there is
> strong reason to consider these two men innocent of the
> crime with which they are charged and for which they have al-
> ready suffered such cruel punishment. Our opinion is shared
> by men and newspapers of very different sympathies and
> parties.
>
> Even if reasons of equity did not exist, we had hoped that
> the sentiment of pity would at least inspire the man who held
> in his hands the fate of these two condemned men. One can
> say only that it is with astonishment that we learned his deci-
> sion, and that in making it he has assumed a heavy moral
> responsibility.

The same paper on August 11:

> If this was not a serious matter one would be tempted to
> describe it as cinematographic justice. Right to the end it has
> shown an extraordinary mixture of melodrama such as would
> have been accounted all but impossible if recounted in fiction.
>
> But the matter is serious from many points of view. One
> must be entirely without heart not to be moved by the torture
> of constant uncertainty inflicted upon these two men. Even if
> Sacco and Vanzetti are guilty, they cannot now be executed
> without the suspicion persisting of a great injustice having
> been done.
>
> In every country all over the world it is the hope and wish of
> all men of ordinary humanity that they should now be spared.

The Paris *Temps* (conservative), August 7:

> We wish to see the lives of these men spared, whether they
> are innocent or guilty, because we think that they have suffered
> enough in these seven years of nightmare. But we do not wish

to go further than that. Human life should always be respected, but so also should the justice [of] a free people. We do not wish that today's manifestations should be otherwise interpreted by the American people than as being perfectly respectful to American justice.

Liberté, Paris (nationalist), August 11:

The burial of this deplorable business would be certainly better from every point of view than the burial of the two victims. The symbolic torch which the Statue of Liberty carries in her hand must not be replaced by two half-scorched scarecrows.

The *Quotidien* (Herriot's paper) says the execution would be a crime against humanity:

If Sacco and Vanzetti are executed with them will be buried American justice. We still hope for pity, for humaneness.

The Berlin *Montagspost* publishes a symposium of the views of about a dozen prominent judges and criminal lawyers to all of whom the seven-year delay in the case seems an inexplicable flaw in American judicial methods. All express the belief that the execution ought not be carried out, and it is pointed out that during the last four years 85 percent of the death sentences in Germany have been commuted. Dr. Eberhardt Schmidt, professor of criminal law at Kiel University, writes: "I am opposed to the death penalty on principle, but apart from that I consider that Sacco and Vanzetti should be pardoned because the death sentence is seven years old."

Upton Sinclair

This telegraph was published in The Nation *on August 24, 1927, by novelist and Socialist Party member Upton Sinclair. In 1928, Sinclair published* Boston: A Documentary Novel *about the case.*

Telegraph to The Nation

TO THE EDITOR OF THE NATION

IF SACCO VANZETTI EXECUTED I URGE BOSTON COMMIT-
TEE SUMMON GRAND JURY OF LIBERAL CITIZENS BRING
FORMAL INDICTMENT AGAINST COMMONWEALTH OF
MASSACHUSETTS FOR FIRST DEGREE MURDER JUDGES
SHOULD BE APPOINTED JURY IMPANELED IN REGULAR
FORM COMPLETE TRIAL HELD SUMMONING ALL WITNES-
SES OF BOTH DEFENSE AND PROSECUTION INCLUDING
JUDGE THAYER AND GOVERNOR FULLER THOSE WHO FAIL
TO ATTEND SHOULD BE REPRESENTED BY PROXY EVEN
MORE IMPORTANT THAN SAVING LIVES OF TWO RADICALS
IS NECESSITY OF EDUCATING AMERICAN PEOPLE TO
NATURE OF THE FRAMEUP NOW AN ESTABLISHED FEAT-
URE OF AMERICAN POLICE SYSTEM I BELIEVE THIS PROP-
OSED TRIAL WOULD BE WIDELY REPORTED.

UPTON SINCLAIR

part three:

Law versus Justice

Lyrics by Joan Baez, Music by Ennio Morricone
The Ballad of Sacco and Vanzetti, Part One

"Give to me your tired and your poor
Your huddled masses yearning to breathe free
The wretched refuse of your teeming shore
Send these, the homeless, tempest-tossed to me."
Blessed are the persecuted
And blessed are the pure in heart
Blessed are the merciful
And blessed are the ones who mourn
The step is hard that tears away the roots
And says goodbye to friends and family
The fathers and the mothers weep
The children cannot comprehend
But when there is a promised land
The brave will go and others follow
The beauty of the human spirit
Is the will to try our dreams
And so the masses teemed across the ocean
To a land of peace and hope
But no one heard a voice or saw a light
As they were tumbled onto shore
And none was welcomed by the echo of the phrase
"I lift my lamp beside the golden door."
Blessed are the persecuted
And blessed are the pure in heart
Blessed are the merciful
And blessed are the ones who mourn.

Felix Frankfurter

*Felix Frankfurter was a professor of law at Harvard in
1927, when he published what is widely considered the
most accomplished critique of the case. This is a shorter
version of his original 18,000 word evaluation.*

The Case of Sacco and Vanzetti

For more than six years the Sacco-Vanzetti case has been before
the courts of Massachusetts. In a state where ordinary murder
trials are promptly dispatched such extraordinary delay in itself
challenges attention. The fact is that a long succession of disclo-
sures has aroused interest far beyond the boundaries of Massachusetts and even of the United States, until the case has become
one of those rare *causes célèbres* which are of international
concern. The aim of this paper is to give in the briefest compass
an accurate résumé of the facts of the case from its earliest
stages to its present posture…

So far as the crime is concerned, we are dealing with a conven-
tional case of payroll robbery. At the trial the killing of Parmenter
and Berardelli was undisputed. The only issue was the identity
of the murderers. Were Sacco and Vanzetti two of the assailants
of Parmenter and Berardelli, or were they not?

On this issue there was at the trial a mass of conflicting evidence. Fifty-nine witnesses testified for the commonwealth and

99 for the defendants. The evidence offered by the commonwealth was not the same against both defendants. The theory of the prosecution was that Sacco did the actual shooting while Vanzetti sat in the car as one of the collaborators in a conspiracy to murder. Witnesses testified to having seen both defendants in South Braintree on the morning of April 15; they claimed to recognize Sacco as the man who shot the guard Berardelli and to have seen him subsequently escape in the car. Expert testimony… was offered seeking to connect one of four bullets removed from Berardelli's body with the Colt pistol found on Sacco at the time of his arrest. As to Vanzetti, the commonwealth adduced evidence placing him at the murder car. Moreover, the commonwealth introduced the conduct of the defendants, as evinced by pistols found on their persons and lies admittedly told by them when arrested, as further proof of identification, in that such conduct revealed "consciousness of guilt."

The defense met the commonwealth's eyewitnesses by other eyewitnesses, slightly more numerous and at least as well circumstanced to observe the assailants, who testified that the defendants were not the men they saw. Their testimony was confirmed by witnesses who proved the presence of Sacco and Vanzetti elsewhere at the time of the murder. Other witnesses supported Sacco's testimony that on April 15 — the day that he was away from work — he was in Boston seeing about a passport to Italy, whither he was planning shortly to return to visit his recently bereaved father. The truth of that statement was supported by an official of the Italian consulate in Boston who deposed that Sacco visited his consulate at an hour that made it impossible for him to have been one of the Braintree murder gang. The claim of Vanzetti that on April 15 he was pursuing his customary trade as fish-peddler was sustained by a number of witnesses who had been his customers that day.

From this summary it must be evident that the trustworthiness

of the testimony which placed Sacco and Vanzetti in South Braintree on April 15 is the foundation of the case...

What is the worth of identification testimony even when uncontradicted? The identification of strangers is proverbially untrust-
worthy...

In the Sacco-Vanzetti case the elements of uncertainty were
intensified. All the identifying witnesses were speaking from cas-
ual observation of men they had never seen before, men of foreign
race, under circumstances of unusual confusion. Thus, one witness, Cole, "thought at the first glance that the man was a Portu-
guese fellow named Tony that he knew." Afterward he was sure
it was Vanzetti. Nor can we abstain from comment on the methods pursued by the police in eliciting subsequent identification.
The recognized procedure is to line up the suspect with others,
and so far as possible with individuals of the same race and
class, so as not to provoke identification through accentuation.
In defiance of these necessary safeguards, Sacco and Vanzetti
after their arrest were shown singly to persons brought there for
the purposes of identification, not as part of a "parade." Moreover,
Sacco and Vanzetti were not even allowed to be their natural
selves; they were compelled to simulate the behavior of the Braintree bandits. Under such conditions identification of foreigners is
a farce.

After the conviction Judge Thayer himself abandoned the identification of Sacco and Vanzetti as the ground on which the jury's
verdict rested... The evidence that convicted these defendants
was circumstantial and was evidence that is known in law as
"consciousness of guilt."

"Consciousness of guilt" meant that the conduct of Sacco
and Vanzetti after April 15 was the conduct of murderers. This
inference of guilt was drawn from their behavior on the night of
May 5, before and after arrest, and also from their possession of
firearms. It is vital to keep in mind the evidence on which,

according to Judge Thayer, these two men are to be sentenced to death. There was no claim whatever at the trial, and none has ever been suggested since, that Sacco and Vanzetti had any prior experience in holdups or any previous association with ban-dits; no claim that the $16,000 taken from the victims ever found its way into their pockets; no claim that their financial condition or that of Sacco's family (he had a wife and child, and another child was soon to be born) was in any way changed after April 15; no claim that after the murder either Sacco or Vanzetti changed his manner of living or employment. Neither of these men had ever been accused of crime before their arrest. Nor did they during the three weeks between the murder and their arrest behave like men who were concealing the crime of murder. They did not go into hiding; they did not abscond with the spoils; they did not live under assumed names. They maintained their old lodgings; they pursued openly their callings within a few miles of the town where they were supposed to have committed murder in broad daylight; and when arrested Sacco was found to have in his pocket an announcement of a forthcoming meeting at which Vanzetti was to speak. Was this the behavior of men eluding identification?...

In statements made to the district attorney and to the chief of police at the police station after their arrest, both Sacco and Vanzetti lied. By misstatements they tried to conceal their move-ments on the day of their arrest, the friends they had been to see, the places they had visited...

What of this evidence of "consciousness of guilt"? The testi-mony of the police that Sacco and Vanzetti were about to draw pistols was emphatically denied by them... If Sacco and Vanzetti were the holdup men of Braintree, why did they not draw upon their expert skill and attempt to make their escape by scattering shots? But, not being gunmen, why should Sacco and Vanzetti have carried guns? The possession of firearms in this country has not at all the significance that it would have, say, in England. The extensive carrying of guns by people who are not "gunmen" is a matter of common knowledge. Sacco acquired the habit of carrying a pistol while a nightwatchman in the shoe factory, because, as his employer testified, "nightwatchmen protecting property do have guns." Vanzetti carried a revolver "because it was a very bad time, and I like to have a revolver for self-defense."...

The other evidence from which "consciousness of guilt" was drawn the two Italians admitted. They acknowledged that they behaved in the way described by [prosecution witness] Mrs. Johnson; and freely conceded that when questioned at the police station they told lies. What was their explanation of this conduct? To exculpate themselves of the crime of murder they had to disclose elaborately their guilt of radicalism. In order to meet the significance which the prosecution attached to the incidents at the Johnson house and those following, it became necessary for the defendants to advertise to the jury their offensive radicalism, and thereby to excite the deepest prejudices of a Norfolk County jury picked for its respectability and sitting in judgment upon two men of alien blood and abhorrent philosophy.

Innocent men, it is suggested, do not lie when picked up by the police. But Sacco and Vanzetti knew they were not innocent of the charge on which they supposed themselves arrested, and about which the police interrogated them. For, when apprehended, Sacco and Vanzetti were not confronted with the charge of murder; they were not accused of banditry; they were not given the remotest intimation that the murders of Parmenter and Berardelli were laid at their door. They were told they were arrested as "suspicious characters," and the meaning which that carried to their minds was rendered concrete by the questions that were put to them.

Q: Tell us all you recall that Stewart, the chief, asked of you.

A: He asked me why we were in Bridgewater, how long I knew

> Sacco, if I am a radical, if I am an anarchist or communist, and he asked me if I believe in the government of the United States.
>
> Q: Did either Chief Stewart at the Brockton police station or Mr. Katzmann tell you that you were suspected of robberies and murder?
>
> A: No

...Plainly their arrest meant to Sacco and Vanzetti arrest for radicalism.

Boston was one of the worst centers of the lawlessness and hysteria that characterized the campaign of the Department of Justice for the wholesale arrest and deportation of Reds... Sacco and Vanzetti were notorious Reds. They were associates of leading radicals; they had for some time been on the list of suspects of the Department of Justice; and they were especially obnoxious because they were draft-dodgers.

The terrorizing methods of the government had very specific meaning for the two Italians. Two of their friends had already been deported. The arrest of the New York radical Salsedo, and his detention incommunicado by the Department of Justice, had been for some weeks a source of great concern to them. Vanzetti was sent to New York to confer with a committee in charge of the case of Salsedo and other Italian political prisoners. On his return, May 2, he reported to his Boston friends the advice which had been given him: namely, to dispose of their radical literature and thus eliminate the most damaging evidence in the deportation proceedings they feared. The urgency of acting on this advice was intensified by the tragic news of Salsedo's death after Vanzetti's return from New York. Though Salsedo's death was unexplained, to Sacco and Vanzetti it conveyed only one explanation. It was a symbol of their fears and an omen of their own fate.

On the witness stand Sacco and Vanzetti accounted for their movements on April 15. They also accounted for their ambiguous behavior on May 5. Up to the time that Sacco and Vanzetti testified to their radical activities, their pacifism, their flight to Mexico to avoid the draft, the trial was a trial for murder and banditry; with the cross-examination of Sacco and Vanzetti, patriotism and radicalism became the dominant emotional issues. Outside the courtroom the Red hysteria was rampant; it was allowed to dominate within. The prosecutor systematically played on the feelings of the jury by exploiting the unpatriotic and despised beliefs of Sacco and Vanzetti, and the judge allowed him thus to divert and pervert the jury's mind...

The function of a judge's charge is to enable the jury to find its way through the maze of conflicting testimony, to sift the relevant from the irrelevant, to weigh wisely, and to judge dispassionately... By his summing up a judge reveals his estimate of relative importance. Judge Thayer's charge directs the emotions only too clearly. What guidance does he give to the mind? The charge occupies 24 pages; of these, 14 are consumed in abstract legal generalities and moral exhortations. Having allowed the minds of the jurors to be impregnated with war feeling, Judge Thayer now invited them to breathe "a purer atmosphere of unyielding impartiality and absolute fairness." Unfortunately the passion and prejudice instilled during the course of a long trial cannot be exorcised by the general, placid language of a charge after the mischief is done. Every experienced lawyer knows that it is idle to ask jurors to dismiss from their memory what has been deposited in their feelings.

In this case the vital issue was identification. That the whole mass of conflicting identification testimony is dismissed in two pages out of 24 is a fair measure of the distorted perspective in which the judge placed the case. He dealt with identification in abstract terms and without mentioning the name of any witness on either side. The alibi testimony he likewise dismissed in two paragraphs, again without reference to specific witnesses. In striking contrast to this sterile treatment of the issue of whether or not Sacco and Vanzetti were in South Braintree on April 15 was his concrete and elaborate treatment of the inferences which might be drawn from the character of their conduct on the night of their arrest. Five pages of the charge are given over to "consciousness of guilt," set forth in great detail and with specific mention of the testimony given by the various police officials and by Mr. and Mrs. Johnson. The disproportionate consideration which Judge Thayer gave to this issue, in the light of his comments during the trial, must have left the impression that the case turned on "consciousness of guilt." As we have seen, Judge Thayer himself did in fact so interpret the jury's verdict afterward...

Hitherto the methods pursued by the prosecution, which explain the convictions, rested on inferences, however compelling. But recently facts have been disclosed, and not denied by the prosecution, to indicate that the case against these Italians for murder was part of a collusive effort between the district attorney and agents of the Department of Justice to rid the country of Sacco and Vanzetti because of their Red activities. In proof of this we have the affidavits of two former officers of the government, one of whom served as post office inspector for 25 years, and both of whom are now in honorable civil employment. Sacco's and Vanzetti's names were on the files of the Department of Justice "as radicals to be watched"; the department was eager for their deportation, but had not evidence enough to secure it; and inasmuch as the U.S. District Court for Massachusetts had checked abuses in deportation proceedings, the department had become chary of resorting to deportation without adequate legal basis. The arrest of Sacco and Vanzetti, on the mistaken theory of Chief Stewart, furnished the agents of the department their opportunity. Although the opinion of the agents working on the case was that "the South Braintree crime was the work of professionals," and that Sacco and Vanzetti, "although anarchists and agitators, were not highway robbers, and had nothing to do with the South Braintree crime," yet they collaborated with the district attorney in the prosecution of Sacco and Vanzetti for murder. For "it was the opinion of the department agents here that a conviction of Sacco and Vanzetti for murder would be one way of disposing of these two men." Here, to be sure, is a startling allegation. But it is made by a man of long years of important service in the government's employ. It is supported by the now admitted installation of a government spy in a cell adjoining Sacco's with a view to "obtaining whatever incriminating evidence he could... after winning his confidence"; by the insinuation of an "undercover man" into the councils of the Sacco-Vanzetti Defense Committee; by the proposed placement of another spy as a lodger in Mrs. Sacco's house; and by the supplying of information about the radical activities of Sacco and Vanzetti to the district attorney by the agents of the Department of Justice.

These joint labors between Boston agents of the Department of Justice and the district attorney led to a great deal of correspondence between the agent in charge and the district attorney and to reports between the agents of the department and Washington. These records have not been made available, nor has their absence been accounted for. An appeal to Attorney General Sargent proved fruitless, although supported by Senator Butler of Massachusetts, requesting that Mr. West, the then agent in charge, "be authorized to talk with counsel for Sacco and Vanzetti and to disclose whatever documents and correspondence are on file in his office dealing with the investigation made by the Boston agents before, during, and after the trial of Sacco and Vanzetti." The facts upon which this appeal was made stand uncontradicted. West made no denial whatever and the district attorney only emphasized his failure to deny the facts charged by the two former agents of the Department of Justice by an affidavit confined to a denial of some of the statements of a former government spy. The charge that the principal agent of the Department of Justice in Boston and the district attorney collaborated to secure the conviction of Sacco and Vanzetti is denied neither by the agent nor by the district attorney. Chief Stewart of Bridgewater takes it upon himself to say that the officials of the department "had nothing whatsoever to do with the preparation of this case for trial." Instead of making a full disclosure of the facts, the representative of the commonwealth indulged in vituperation against the former officers of the Department of Justice as men who were guilty of "a breach of loyalty" because they violated the watch word of the Department of Justice, "Do not betray the secrets of your departments." To which Mr. Thompson rightly replies, "What are the secrets which they admit?... A government which has come to value its own secrets more than it does the lives of its citizens has become a tyranny... Secrets, secrets! And he says you should abstain from touching this verdict of your jury because it is so sacred. Would they not have liked to know something about the secrets? The case is admitted by that inadvertent concession. There are, then, secrets to be admitted." Yet Judge Thayer found in these circumstances only opportunity to make innuendo against a former official of the government well known for his long and honorable service, and an elaborate denial of a claim that was never made. Not less than 12 times Judge Thayer ridicules the charge of a conspiracy between "these two great governments — that of the United States and the Commonwealth of Massachusetts!" He indulges in much patriotic protestation, but is wholly silent about the specific acts of wrongdoing and lawlessness connected with the Red Raids of 1920. The historian who relied on this opinion would have to assume that the charge of lawlessness and misconduct in the deportations of outlawed radicals was the traitorous invention of a diseased mind.

The verdict of guilty was brought in on July 14, 1921. The exceptions which had been taken to rulings at the trial were made

the basis of an application for a new trial, which Judge Thayer refused. Subsequently a great mass of new evidence was un-
earthed by the defense, and made the subject of other motions
for a new trial, all heard before Judge Thayer and all denied by
him. The hearing on the later motions took place on October 1,
1923, and was the occasion of the entry into the case of Mr.
William G. Thompson, a powerful advocate bred in the traditions
of the Massachusetts courts. The espousal of the Sacco-Vanzetti
cause by a man of Mr. Thompson's professional prestige at once
gave it a new complexion and has been its mainstay ever since.
For he has brought to the case, not only his great ability as a
lawyer, but the strength of his conviction that these two men are
innocent and that their trial was not characterized by those high
standards which are the pride of Massachusetts justice.

We have now reached a stage of the case the details of which
shake one's confidence in the whole course of the proceedings...
Vital to the identification of Sacco and Vanzetti as the murderers
was the identification of one of the fatal bullets as a bullet coming
from Sacco's pistol. The evidence excluded the possibility that
five other bullets found in the dead bodies were fired by either
Sacco or Vanzetti. When Judge Thayer placed the case in the
jury's hands for judgment he charged them that the commonwealth had introduced the testimony of two experts, Proctor and
Van Amburgh, to the effect that the fatal bullet went through
Sacco's pistol...

After the conviction Proctor in an affidavit swore to the following
account of his true views and the manner in which they were
phrased for purposes of the trial:

> At the trial, the district attorney did not ask me whether I had
> found evidence that the so-called mortal bullet which I have
> referred to as Number Three passed through Sacco's pistol,
> nor was I asked that question on cross-examination. The dis-
> trict attorney desired to ask me that question, but I had repeat-

edly told him that if he did I should be obliged to answer in the negative; consequently, he put to me this question: Q. Have you an opinion as to whether bullet Number Three was fired from the Colt automatic which is in evidence? To which I answered, 'I have.' He then proceeded: Q. And what is your opinion? A. My opinion is that it is consistent with being fired by that pistol...

But I do not intend by that answer to imply that I had found any evidence that the so-called mortal bullet had passed through this particular Colt automatic pistol and the district attorney well knew that I did not so intend and framed his question accordingly...

This affidavit of Proctor was the basis of Mr. Thompson's motion for a new trial before Judge Thayer...

On May 12, 1926, the Supreme Court of Massachusetts found "no error" in any of the rulings of Judge Thayer. The guilt or innocence of the defendants was not retried in the Supreme Court. That court could not inquire whether the facts as set forth in the printed record justified the verdict. Such would have been the scope of judicial review had the case come before the New York Court of Appeals or the English Court of Criminal Appeal. In those jurisdictions a judgment upon the facts as well as upon the law is open, and their courts decide whether convictions should stand in view of the whole record. A much more limited scope in reviewing connections prevails in Massachusetts. What is reviewed in effect is the conduct of the trial judge; only so-called questions of law are open.

The merits of the legal questions raised by the exceptions cannot be discussed here. Suffice it to say, with deference, that some of the Supreme Court rulings are puzzling in the extreme...

The Supreme Court of Massachusetts will be called upon to search the whole record in order to determine whether Judge Thayer duly observed the traditional standards of fairness and reason which govern the conduct of an Anglo-American judge, particularly in a capital case. This court has given us the requirements by which Judge Thayer's decision is to be measured and the tests which it will use in determining whether a new trial shall be granted:

> The various statements of the extent of the power and of limitations upon the right to grant new trials... must yield to the fundamental test, in aid of which most rules have been formulated, that such motions ought not to be granted unless on a survey of the whole case it appears to the judicial conscience and judgment that otherwise a miscarriage of justice will result.
>
> Nor must a new trial be withheld where in justice it is called for, because thereby encouragement will be given to improper demands for a new trial. For, as the Chief Justice of Massachusetts has announced, courts cannot close "their eyes to injustice on account of facility of abuse."

With these legal canons as a guide, the outcome ought not to be in doubt.

Source: For the full text of Felix Frankfurter's essay on the case, see *The Atlantic Monthly*: http:www.theatlantic.com/unbound/flashbks/oj/frankff.htm

A Correspondent to *The Nation*

"A correspondent" wrote this article for the
August 13, 1927, edition of The Nation.

An American Tragedy

No journalistic pen could do justice to the tragic incidents and implications of the great Massachusetts case, which, as these lines are being set up, is being rushed to its fatal conclusion. The character of its place in history can hardly now be a matter of dispute. The affair of Sacco and Vanzetti belongs to the momentous criminal trials of the world. It stands by itself in the annals of the United States, of the English-speaking world. It will affect the reputation of America among the peoples of Europe certainly during the lifetime of the present generation. Directly or indirectly it will lead to changes in the criminal law and legal procedure of America. Throughout the civilized world it will influence the popular mind in relation to the ethics of capital punishment, and will play its part in that movement toward the drastic reform of the police system which, urgently necessary in every country, is, by the admission of all informed persons, especially and clamorously overdue in the United States. The guilt or innocence of Sacco and Vanzetti may never be absolutely determined. Through their trial and fate they have become historic.

It is manifest that in the presence of the completed tragedy no good purpose could be served by a restatement of the issues of the affair or a recapitulation of the events of the final sensational stage; but a few points may here be specifically noted.

Moved by the weight of public opinion in favor of a reopening of the case, the governor of Massachusetts at the end of May appointed a special commission of three to review the record of the case, Dr. Lawrence Lowell, president of Harvard University, being associated with two other well-known citizens. Their task was to review the printed record of the case, which fills some 7,000 pages of testimony, argument and opinion. They were not entrusted with the duty of examining fresh witnesses: that was undertaken by Governor Fuller himself. The hearings were held in private. Counsel for the prisoners were not present. One week only before the date finally fixed for the execution the commission reported to the effect that the prisoners had received a fair trial and there was no ground for a new trial. The governor affirmed his agreement with that finding, stated his belief that the guilt of the men had been proved and announced that the execution must take place. Refusing even then to accept defeat, counsel for the defense made one more desperate motion for a new trial. It was heard and dismissed in circumstances of an extraordinarily tragic irony, emphasizing what is to English students the most singular aspect of the whole affair. The judge who heard the application and refused it, was the same Judge Webster Thayer who had presided over the sessions trial, directed the jury to the verdict of guilty, pronounced the death sentence, heard and rejected every subsequent application, and exerted himself during the revision inquiry to make certain the fulfillment of his judgment. In the State of Massachusetts the judge who tries a prisoner on a capital charge is not only permitted to act as the Court of Appeal upon himself, he is required to do so. There is reason to believe that the system which makes this procedure regular in Massachusetts will not long survive the case which has brought it to the astonished attention of the world; but the seven-year struggle for the lives of Sacco and Vanzetti was governed by it from beginning to end.

There cannot be any parallel to the most remarkable struggle carried on by the voluntary defense committee organized in Boston. The full story will one day be told, and it will then be recognized as possessing a heroic quality. It would be impossible to imagine a more hopeless cause than that of the two men accused in 1920 of the South Braintree murders. They were Italians, aliens and anarchists: that is to say, they were members of the most despised section of the variegated immigrant community of America, and were associated with the most hated tenets. They were known to have been active in the work of spreading their subversive creed. They were arrested at a time of excessive panic, when with the support of public opinion the authorities were engaged in harrying suspect aliens of almost every nationality. One of the two accused was being charged with complicity in another crime. Both had been "draft-dodgers," having as aliens run away from the conscription law. After their arrest they had lied to the police, in fear of torture and in the knowledge of what had happened to some of their fellows in the anti-alien campaign. The case against them looked altogether black; and the public temper was such that no good American could associate himself with their cause without the certainty of losing caste, and most probably being made to suffer seriously in pocket. It was amid such conditions as these that the agitation for the defense of Sacco and Vanzetti was begun.

The original committee formed for the purpose of organizing the defense consisted almost or altogether of Italians, apparently without distinction of political creed. Indeed, it was noticeable as the affair went on that the Boston branch of the Fascisti had come to the support of the committee, the nationalism of its members, reinforced by resentment against the 100 percent American attitude toward the alien, being strong enough in this instance to override the fascist hatred of revolutionary ideas. Upon this Italian committee, at any rate in the earlier stages, fell the heavier part of the work of enlisting legal and financial aid for the defense. But it is the strictly American element in the defense agitation that has proved to be the more original and striking. The first active steps were taken by certain labor and other radical speakers, who, interpreting the arrest of Sacco and Vanzetti in the light of many incidents of the time, called pointed attention to suspicious circumstances in the action of the police and legal authorities in Massachusetts. Their advocacy made an impression upon a number of well-known Boston liberals, men and women, who, being convinced that the case against the accused was a police "frame-up," went in the defense from pure love of justice and in concern for the honor of the courts and the commonwealth. They watched it through all its stages. They attended in relays the court at Dedham, day by day throughout the seven weeks of the sessions' trial in the summer of 1921. They made friends with the reporters, and thus obtained knowledge of the judge and jury not accessible from the visitors' seats in the courtroom. When the trial ended in the fatal verdict they set to work to establish a regular and permanent organization for the defense, in order that no means of delaying the death sentence might be neglected. Their hope was that a further quantity of favorable evidence might be assembled, and the case be reopened amid circumstances, both in the courts and outside, free from the hysterical passions that had prevailed in 1920 and 1921. The labor was difficult beyond description, and by its very nature it was heartbreaking. The cause, insofar as it was known to the public, was exceedingly unpopular; while the prisoners, kept in separate jails, endured an experience which, varied only by spells of sickness and insanity, exceeded the bitterness of death. Massachusetts, relatively speaking, has a record of quick dealing with criminal cases; but it was found possible to bring about one postponement after another. Very large sums of money were needed, and were collected. An extraordinary movement of publicity was organized and maintained, so that in the course of a few years the case of Sacco and Vanzetti was known to every newspaper of the United States and in some degree to the press of the world. Eminent lawyers offered their services, not the least notable fact in this connection being this, that several of them belonged to the exclusive section of the conservative professional community of Old Boston — a community which for generations had been habitually described as of Brahminical exclusiveness and tenacity. In the presentation of the case through the press of England and America the statement has been repeatedly made that the agitation on behalf of Sacco and Vanzetti was labor and communist. The whole point of the remarkable body of protest, gathering steadily in weight and volume year after year, is that it came from the general public, under the leadership of jurists and professors of law, leading churchmen, men of letters and independent citizens, belonging to every department of American life. From the single fact that, two months before the end, a petition containing nearly half a million names was presented to the governor of Massachusetts, we may realize in some measure the national effect of the prolonged agitation for a reopening of the case. One thing at least in this connection may surely be said: that this vast disinterested effort by her private citizens to further the cause of justice and mercy should be remembered to the glory of Massachusetts, long after her judicial system has been purged of the defects which have been thrown into such somber relief by the tragic case of Sacco and Vanzetti.

John Dos Passos

This letter by novelist John Dos Passos was published in The Nation, *August 1927, after an advisory committee appointed by Governor Fuller and headed by Harvard President A. Lawrence Lowell declared that there was no need for a new trial.*

An Open Letter to President Lowell

Boston, August 9
To the Editor of The Nation

SIR: I am asking the courtesy of your columns for the enclosed open letter to President Lowell of Harvard that no publication in Boston seems willing to publish.

As a graduate of Harvard University I feel that I have the right to protest against the participation of the president of that university in the report on the Sacco-Vanzetti case presented to Governor Fuller by his advisory committee. I feel that you have put your name and indirectly the name of the university you represent to an infamous document. This is no time for mincing words. You have made yourself a party to a judicial murder that will call down on its perpetrators the execration of the civilized world. What it means is that you are allowing a Massachusetts politician to use the name of Harvard to cover his own bias and to whitewash all the dirty business of the arrest of these men at the time of the anarchist raids and their subsequent slow torture by the spiteful and soulless mechanism of the law. They have probably told you that this was a mere local decision on a Boston murder case, but to any man with enough intelligence to read the daily papers it must be clear that somehow it has ceased being a Boston murder case. Sacco and Vanzetti starving in their cells in the death house and the authorities of the State of Massachusetts building the electric chair in which to burn them to death have become huge symbols on the stage of the world. The part into which you have forced Harvard University will make many a man ashamed of being one of its graduates.

Many of us who have watched the case for years felt that your appointment as a member of the committee assured at least a modicum of fair play and of historical perspective in the conduct of the investigation. This hope was pretty well shattered when it was announced that the investigation was to be carried on behind closed doors. If there was nothing to hide, why the secrecy? Since when have star chamber proceedings been part of the American judicial system?

The published report has confirmed our worst forebodings. With inconceivable levity you counsel the electrocution of two men because it "seems" to you that the enormous mass of evidence piled up by the defense in seven years' heartbreaking work should be dismissed, like the rent in the lining of the cap that you wrongly assert fitted Sacco, as so trifling a matter in the evidence of the case that it seems to the committee by no means a ground for a new trial. Did the committee feel that the prosecution's case was so weak that they had to bolster it by fresh deductions and surmises of their own?

The report in its entirety is an apology for the conduct of the trial rather than an impartial investigation. Reading it, the suspicion grows paragraph by paragraph that its aim was not to review but to make respectable the proceedings of Judge Thayer and the district attorney's office. Not in a single phrase is there an inkling of a sense on your part or on that of your colleagues of the importance of the social and racial backgrounds of the trial. Your loose use of the words "socialistic" and "communistic" prove that you are ignorant or careless of the differences in mentality involved in partisanship in the various schools of revolutionary thought.

This is a matter of life and death, not only for Sacco and Vanzetti but for the civilization that Harvard University is supposed to represent. The Sacco-Vanzetti case has become part of the world struggle between the capitalist class and the working class, between those who have power and those who are struggling to get it. In a man in high office, ignorance of the new sprouting forces that are remaking society, whether he is with them or against them, is little short of criminal. It is inconceivable that intelligent reading men can be ignorant in this day of the outlines of anarchist philosophy. Instead of crying ignorance, it would be franker to admit that as anarchists and agitators you hate these men and disapprove of their ideas and methods. But are you going to sacrifice the integrity of the legal system to that feeling? Are you going to prove by a bloody reprisal that the radical contention that a man holding unpopular ideas cannot get a free trial in our courts is true?

I cannot feel that either you or your colleagues have understood the full purport of your decision. If you had you would certainly have made out a more careful case for yourselves, one less full of loopholes and contradictions. It is upon men of your class and position that will rest the inevitable decision as to whether the coming struggle for the reorganization of society shall be bloodless and fertile or inconceivably bloody and destructive. It is high time that you realized the full extent of the responsibility on your shoulders.

As a Harvard man I want to protest most solemnly against your smirching the university of which you are an officer with the foul crime against humanity and civilization to which you have made yourself accessory.

H.G. Wells

Novelist and historian H.G. Wells was involved in the campaign in Britain. This piece was refused publication when written in 1927, and eventually appeared in Wells's collection of essays, The Way The World is Going, *in 1929.*

Outrages in Defense of Order
The Proposed Murder of Two American Radicals

...After reading Professor Frankfurter's book through I went to and fro in it, picking out everything I could about Judge Thayer. My curiosity grows. I would like to study him intensively, get photographs of him, dive into his life story, learn about his school and college. And that, not because I think he is anything strange and out of the way, but because he is so tremendously normal. I perceive that he was in perfect accord with the district attorney, Katzmann, and in close sympathy with the jury, when Sacco and Vanzetti were not so much tried as baited in his court. He had no feeling of wrongdoing at that time. "Thayerism," if he will permit me to draw a word from him, is no rare thing, in America. Nor is it rare in England. It interweaves intimately with the mental quality of the European fascist. It is a widely diffused and dangerous force in our modern world. "Thayerism," the self-righteous unrighteousness of established people. Let us consider its more salient characteristics.

In the first place, after my first exploration of Judge Thayer, I am left with the persuasion that he is, legally speaking, a quite honest man. That is to say, I do not think that he was guided by any considerations of personal profit to take the line of conduct that is making him *stupor mundi*, the amazement of the civilized world. I think that he and his jurymen had a feeling of profound obligation to their country, and that they really supposed that they were serving great civilized ideals in doing as they did in the conviction of their victims. I am not so sure of the district attorney. I thought his cross-examination tricky and evil; but then I am accustomed to the candors of science, and I find most lawyers in most cross-examinations tricky and evil. But district attorney apart, the court, I am convinced, felt that it was making a large fair display and doing helpful work to maintain the good life, the spacious and generous and wholesome American life, by accepting proofs that were no proofs against these friendless men — who "deserved to be hanged anyway." I feel sure that the judge went home to his family — and I can quite believe he has a very nice family — with a sense of a stern duty manfully done.

After the trial I agree that his record is not so straightforward. The criticism of his verdict seems to have surprised and hurt him. He must have felt that he had settled this business for his country's good, and that he did not deserve the trouble made about his settlement. His conduct suggests wounded vanity and bad temper rather than any satanic qualities. People came into court and hurt his feelings by motions for a new trial, which he refused indignantly. The Supreme Judicial Court of Massachusetts, without inquiry into the evidence of the murder, but simply upon legal issues, upheld his right to block a retrial. It still upholds him. To the last application based upon the Madeiros confession of 1925, after studying the motion "for several weeks without interruption," he produced an opinion of 25,000 words. Professor Frankfurter describes it, with manifest deliberation of phrase and with all the weight of a trained critic of just this sort of material, as "a farrago of misquotations, misrepresentations, suppressions and mutilation." I quote without endorsement this opinion.

I believe Judge Thayer's conduct of the original case was entirely honest; and if his final opinion hardly comes up to the standards of that high word, it still remains, for most fallible men, a very human and sympathetic effort. What is the matter with Judge Thayer is not that he is a bad man, not that he is antimoral, but that he is — to put it mildly — extremely obtuse mentally and morally. This mental and moral obtuseness seems to have extended to his court and to a considerable body of opinion in the United States which sustained him in his crushing of these two unfortunates.

It is difficult to say just how far that obtuseness does not extend in our English-speaking communities. Many people in the continent of Europe hold that it is innate, that the American and English are by nature stupid people, acting often with clumsy and unintentional cruelty, and missing the point of most issues. That stupidity carries with it a certain obduracy which in many rough practical issues has the effect of strength. But the writing and acts of Judge Thayer and his district attorney indicate considerable acuteness and liveliness. I do not believe they are naturally dishonest or stupid. I am quite willing to credit them with intelligence, integrity and public spirit. But it is crude intelligence, dull integrity and sentimental public spirit. They have underdeveloped minds; the minds of lumpish overgrown children. They have had no fine moral and intellectual training. They have lived in an atmosphere where there is no subtle criticism of conduct and opinion, where everything is black or white, bad "to be hanged anyway," or good to be given every privilege. Everything is overemphasized. To be bad or wrong is not to be against the law on this issue or that; it is to be outlawed and not given a dog's chance. It is to be hounded down. They have acquired no pride in discrimination or exactitude. They are easily prejudiced violently for or against anything, and they are as incapable of behaving with scrupulous fairness to anyone who they think is in the wrong as they are capable of the sloppiest adulation and indulgence for anyone they think is in the right. In religion they have never learnt to distinguish cant from faith, they are the natural prey of Elmer Gantry and his kind, and in politics and social questions they cannot distinguish honest criticism of their fundamental ideas from aimless malignant wickedness. They are not mentally quickened to the point of generosity; they are blind to the pathetic idealism of these poor aliens in their midst; they have panics against dreaming workmen who can scarcely talk intelligibly; they see red and feel murderous. And they mean well!

They mean well. That is the tragedy of this situation. The Judge Thayers of our world, just as much as the Saccos and Vanzettis, want the world to be fair and fine. The motives on neither side are entirely base. But Thayerism has the upper hand, and it is all too ready for hasty conclusions even if they involve blood sacrifices. Too many Americans, I fear, believe that a little bloodletting is good for their civilization. So did the Aztecs before them. But blood is a poor cement for the foundations of a civilization. It is less a cement than a corrosive. There have been civilizations before the present one in America, and for all the blood they shed so abundantly upon their high places they have gone and are buried and stuff for the archaeologist.

Six weeks still remain for justice and pity. Will the mighty and fortunate United States, perhaps the greatest power in the world today, allow the State of Massachusetts to kill this machine hand and this fish-peddler on the charge that they have committed a crime of which all the world now knows them innocent, or will it, at the 11th hour, induce the governor of that state to put an end to their seven years of misery and hardship in some more gracious fashion?

part four:

The Legacy

John Dos Passos
*Eulogy for Sacco and Vanzetti: **"They Are Dead Now"***

This isn't a poem
This is two men in grey prison clothes.
One man sits looking at the sick flesh of his hands—hands that
    haven't worked for seven years.
Do you know how long a year is?
Do you know how many hours there are in a day
when a day is twenty-three hours on a cot in a cell,
in a cell in a row of cells in a tier of rows of cells
all empty with the choked emptiness of dreams?
Do you know the dreams of men in jail?
They are dead now
The black automatons have won.
They are burned up utterly
their flesh has passed into the air of Massachuse
    dreams have passed into the wind.
"They are dead now," the Governor's secretary r
    the Governor,
"They are dead now," the Superior Court Judge
    the Supreme Court Judge,
"They are dead now" the College President nud
    the College President
A dry chuckling comes up from all the dead:
The white collar dead; the silk-hatted dead;
the frockcoated dead
They hop in and out of automobiles
breathe deep in relief
as they walk up and down the Boston streets.
They are free of dreams now
free of greasy prison denim
their voices blow back in a thousand lingoes
singing one song
to burst the eardrums of Massachusetts
Make a poem of that if you dare!

Source: John Dos Passos, "They Are Dead Now—" *New Masses*,
October 1927.

Emma Goldman and Alexander Berkman

Anarchists Emma Goldman and Alexander Berkman were deported in 1919 during the Red Scare. This article was published in the New York anarchist journal Road to Freedom *in August 1929 to commemorate the anniversary of the execution.*

Sacco and Vanzetti

The names of the "good shoemaker and poor fish-peddler" have ceased to represent merely two Italian working men. Throughout the civilized world Sacco and Vanzetti have become a symbol, the shibboleth of Justice crushed by Might. That is the great historic significance of this 20th century crucifixion, and truly prophetic, were the words of Vanzetti when he declared, "The last moment belongs to us — that agony is our triumph."

We hear a great deal of progress and by that people usually mean improvements of various kinds, mostly lifesaving discoveries and laborsaving inventions, or reforms in the social and political life. These may or may not represent a real advance because reform is not necessarily progress.

It is an entirely false and vicious conception that civilization consists of mechanical or political changes. Even the greatest improvements do not, in themselves, indicate real progress: they merely symbolize its results. True civilization, real progress consists in *humanizing* mankind, in making the world a decent place to live in. From this viewpoint we are very far from being civilized, in spite of all the reforms and improvements.

True progress is a struggle against the inhumanity of our social existence, against the barbarity of dominant conceptions. In other words, progress is a spiritual struggle, a struggle to free man from his brutish inheritance, from the fear and cruelty of his primitive condition. Breaking the shackles of ignorance and superstition; liberating man from the grip of enslaving ideas and practices; driving darkness out of his mind and terror out of his heart; raising him from his abject posture to man's full stature — that is the mission of progress. Only thus does man, individually and collectively, become truly civilized and our social life more human and worthwhile.

This struggle marks the real history of progress. Its heroes are not the Napoleons and the Bismarcks, not the generals and politicians. Its path is lined with the unmarked graves of the Saccos and Vanzettis of humanity, dotted with the auto-da-fé, the torture chambers, the gallows and the electric chair. To those martyrs of justice and liberty we owe what little of real progress and civilization we have today.

The anniversary of our comrades' death is therefore by no means an occasion for mourning. On the contrary, we should rejoice that in this time of debasement and degradation, in the hysteria of conquest and gain, there are still MEN that dare defy the dominant spirit and raise their voices against inhumanity and reaction: That there are still men who keep the spark of reason and liberty alive and have the courage to die, and die triumphantly, for their daring.

For Sacco and Vanzetti died, as the entire world knows today, because they were anarchists. That is to say, because they believed and preached human brotherhood and freedom. As such, they could expect neither justice nor humanity. For the Masters of Life can forgive any offense or crime but never an attempt to undermine their security on the backs of the masses. Therefore Sacco and Vanzetti had to die, notwithstanding the protests of the entire world.

Yet Vanzetti was right when he declared that his execution was his greatest triumph, for all through history it has been the martyrs of progress that have ultimately triumphed. Where are the Caesars and Torquemadas of yesterday? Who remembers the names of the judges who condemned Giordano Bruno and John Brown? The Parsons and the Ferrers, the Saccos and Vanzettis live eternal and their spirits still march on.

Let no despair enter our hearts over the graves of Sacco and Vanzetti. The duty we owe them for the crime we have committed in permitting their death is to keep their memory green and the banner of their anarchist ideal high. And let no near-sighted pessimist confuse and confound the true facts of man's history, of his rise to greater manhood and liberty. In the long struggle from darkness to light, in the age-old fight for greater freedom and welfare, it is the rebel, the martyr who has won. Slavery has given way, absolutism is crushed, feudalism and serfdom had to go, thrones have been broken and republics established in their stead. Inevitably, the martyrs and their ideas have triumphed, in spite of gallows and electric chairs. Inevitably, the people, the masses, have been gaining on their masters, till now the very citadels of Might, Capital and the State, are being endangered. Russia has shown the direction of the further progress by its attempt to eliminate both the economic and political master. That initial experiment has failed, as all first great social revaluations require repeated efforts for their realization. But that magnificent historic failure is like unto the martyrdom of Sacco and Vanzetti — the symbol and guarantee of ultimate triumph.

Let it be clearly remembered, however, that the failure of FIRST attempts at fundamental social change is always due to the false method of trying to establish the NEW by OLD means and practices. The NEW can conquer only by means of its own new spirit. Tyranny lives by suppression; liberty thrives on freedom. The fatal mistake of the great Russian Revolution was that it tried to establish new forms of social and economic life on the old foundation of coercion and force. The entire development of human society has been AWAY from coercion and government, away from authority toward greater freedom and independence. In that struggle the spirit of liberty has ultimately won out. In the same direction lies further achievement. All history proves it and Russia is the most convincing recent demonstration of it. Let us then learn that lesson and be inspired to greater efforts in behalf of a new world of humanity and freedom, and may the triumphant martyrdom of Sacco and Vanzetti give us greater strength and endurance in this superb struggle.

Howard Zinn

Historian Howard Zinn wrote this 1978 introduction to Boston, *on the 50th anniversary of the publication of Upton Sinclair's novel on the case. [excerpted]*

Upton Sinclair and Sacco and Vanzetti

...The story of Sacco and Vanzetti, whenever revived, even after half a century, awakens deep feelings. In the summer of 1977, Governor Michael Dukakis of Massachusetts officially pronounced that the two men had not had a fair trial, and immediately there were outcries in the state legislature, letters to the newspapers.

One citizen wrote: "By what incredible arrogance do Governor Dukakis and Daniel A. Taylor, his legal adviser, dare to put themselves above Governor Alvin T. Fuller of Massachusetts, who declared that Sacco and Vanzetti had a fair trial, were fairly convicted and fairly punished for their crime?"

Another, signing his letter "John M. Cabot, U.S. Ambassador, Retired," expressed his "great indignation" and noted that Governor Fuller's affirmation of the death sentence was made after a special review by "three of Massachusetts' most distinguished and respected citizens — President Lowell of Harvard, President Stratton of MIT, and retired Judge Grant."

Heywood Broun put it a bit differently, in his column in the *New York World* 50 years ago: "It is not every prisoner who has a President of Harvard University throw on the switch for him... If this is a lynching, at least the fish-peddler and his friend the factory hand may take unction to their souls that they will die at the hands of men in dinner jackets of academic gowns."

Governor Fuller's son, Peter Fuller, Boston's leading Cadillac dealer, as well as a racer of thoroughbred horses, called Dukakis' statement "an attempt to besmirch a guy's record that we believe in and love, whose memory we cherish." He added: "We're sitting here in the last building my father built, and it's the most beautiful car agency on the Eastern Coast and perhaps in the United States."

In New York, a few days before August 23, 1977, the 50th anniversary of the execution, the *New York Times* reported: "Plans by Mayor Beame to proclaim next Tuesday 'Sacco and Vanzetti Day' have been canceled in an effort to avoid controversy, a City Hall spokesman said yesterday."

There must be a good reason why a case 50 years old, its principals dead, arouses such emotion. It is not the kind of history that can be handled comfortably, in harmless ceremonies, like the bicentennial celebrations of 1976, in which the revolutionary doctrines of the Declaration of Independence were lost in a Disneyland of Pageantry. Sacco and Vanzetti were not Washington and Jefferson, not wealthy insurgents making a half-revolution to replace a foreign ruling class with a native one, to exchange a limited monarchy for a limited democracy. They were... "wops," foreigners, poor working men.

Worst of all, Sacco and Vanzetti were anarchists, meaning they had some crazy notion of a full democracy in which neither foreignness nor poverty would exit, and thought that without those provocations, war among nations would end for all time. But to do this, the rich would have to be fought and their riches confiscated. This is not like killing to rob a payroll. It is a crime much worse, and the story of two such men cannot be recalled without trouble.

Therefore, let us recall it. But let us not concentrate on that question which is the center of most discussion of the Sacco-Vanzetti case: were they guilty of the robbery committed April 15, 1920, at the Slater & Morrill shoe factory in South Braintree, Massachusetts, and the murder of the paymaster Frederick Parmenter, and the guard, Alessandro Berardelli? Let us go beyond that question to ask others, more important, more dangerous.

Not that we can neglect the question of guilt or innocence: the trial, the witnesses, the defendants, the judge, the jury, the lawyers, and all those appeals to the higher courts, the governor, the presidents of Harvard and MIT, to the Supreme Court of the United States. It is, indeed, the suspiciousness surrounding all that which leads us further...

Too many defenders of Sacco and Vanzetti are embarrassed by their radicalism and concentrate on the "who-done-it?" of the robbery-murder. But the determination to get rid of them was too persistently fanatical to be an oddity of Boston or Harvard, an unfortunate judicial slip, a prejudice of one person or another. It is best explained by the powerful resolve of the American capitalist system after World War I to eliminate all radical threats on the eve of a new and uncertain era in world history. This fear of opposition seems exaggerated, knowing the weakness of revolutionary movements in America, but there is considerable historical evidence that the American ruling class, with so much at stake — control of the greatest aggregate wealth in the world — takes no chances...

The war in Europe created an opportunity for a patriotic assault on radical movements. Congress legislated, President Wilson signed, the Supreme Court sanctioned, the Department of Justice moved, and 2,000 dissenters from the war were prosecuted, 900 sent to prison. Virtually the entire leadership of the Industrial Workers of the World (IWW) was put on trial and jailed; the socialist and anarchist movements were crippled by jailings and deportations.

With the war over, the repression did not end; indeed, it intensified, for in the meantime the Bolsheviks had taken power in
Russia. It is hard for us today to understand fully the fright of the
American capitalist class at the event. But if the U.S. Government,
so powerful in the 1960s, could be driven to a frenzy of mass
bombardment by the prospect of a small Asian country turning
communist, it becomes easier to understand the reactions to
the Russian Revolution, as the trial of Julius and Ethel Rosenberg
in 1951 does to the Chinese communist victory two years earlier.

Had not the atmosphere cooled between 1920 (the trial of
Sacco and Vanzetti) and 1927 (their execution)? Somewhat. But
by now the case was a national cause, an international issue. It
had become a test of will, of class strength. We'll show them!
"Did you see what I did to those anarchistic bastards the other
day? That will hold them for a while." (The words of Judge Thayer,
spoken at a Dartmouth football game after he had turned down a
defense motion for a new trial, quoted in an affidavit by Dartmouth
Professor James Richardson.)

The American system keeps control not only by a lottery of
rewards (only a few make it, but everyone has a chance), but
also by a lottery of punishments (only a few are put away or
killed, but it's better to play it safe, be quiet). The determination
to get a few obscure communists, or a few obscure Italian anarchists, only becomes comprehensible as part of such a system,
a scheme only partly understood by those who carry it out, but
with the accumulation of more than enough parts to make the
plan whole. What is perhaps not seen at all by jury, and only
dimly by the prosecutor, is seen more clearly by Governor Fuller,
the wealthy auto dealer, and Lowell, the textile-millionaire president of Harvard...

...Expectations of "justice" become as naive as expectations
of winning at roulette, for in both cases, while there are rare
exceptions, to keep suckers coming, the structure of the game
insures that everyone will be kept in place. If a case like that of

Sacco and Vanzetti is seen, not as an objective weighing of evidence, but as an instance of the struggle between the classes, then Sacco's insistence from the beginning, waving aside all lawyers' promises and friends' hopes, makes profound sense: "They got us, they will kill us." So does his statement to the court, on sentencing: "I know the sentence will be between two classes, the oppressed class and the rich class... That is why I am here today on the bench, for having been of the oppressed class."

That viewpoint seems dogmatic, simplistic. Not all court decisions are explained by it. But, lacking a theory to fit *all* cases, Sacco's simple, strong view is surely a better guide to understanding the legal system than one which assumes a contest among equals based on an objective search for truth.

Then on whom can the Saccos and Vanzettis of our time depend, when the judicial system, however frocked to disguise its shape, is made of the same stuff as the larger system to which it connects?...

Vanzetti had the answer. Unless a million Americans were organized, he and his friend Sacco would die. Not legal arguments, only mass action could save them. Not words, but struggles. Not appeals, but demands. Not petitions to the governor, but takeover of the factories. Not lubricating the machinery of a supposedly fair system, to make it work better, but a general strike to bring the machinery to a halt.

That never happened. Thousands demonstrated, marched, protested, not just in Union Square, Boston, Chicago, San Francisco, but in London, Paris, Buenos Aires, South Africa. It wasn't enough. In the 1960s, when a great national movement against Vietnam War was created, involving millions of people, the vibrations shook some courts, some juries, into acquittals for political defendants. But there was no such mass movement for Sacco and Vanzetti.

Still, Vanzetti's idea held. If people struggled, organized, understood that it was not a court case, but an epic encounter, then, even if two men died, something good would come out of it. As Vanzetti told a reporter in the last days, foreseeing the effect: "This is our agony, and our triumph." Indeed, Americans of every generation since that time have learned, and some become more radical, by the recollection of the case of Sacco and Vanzetti.

When Vanzetti was arrested, he had a leaflet in his pocket, advertising a meeting to take place in five days. It is a leaflet that could be distributed today, all over the world, as appropriate now as it was the day of their arrest. It read:

"You have fought all the wars. You have worked for all the capitalists. You have wandered over all the countries. Have you harvested the fruits of your labors, the price of your victories? Does the past comfort you? Does the present smile on you? Does the future promise you anything? Have you found a piece of land where you can live like a human being and die like a human being? On these questions, on this argument and on this theme, the struggle for existence, Bartolomeo Vanzetti will speak."

That meeting did not take place. But Vanzetti did speak, and so did Sacco, over the years of their imprisonment, in their letters, in their legacy, in the literature carrying their message, their spirit forward. As in Upton Sinclair's extraordinary book, *Boston*.

Juliet Ucelli

Juliet Ucelli of Italian Americans for a Multicultural United States gave this speech at a rally on the 75th anniversary of Sacco and Vanzetti's execution, on August 23, 2002, in New York.

Speech Commemorating the 75th Anniversary of Sacco and Vanzetti's Death

I would like to briefly address the lessons of Sacco's and Vanzetti's lives and deaths for Italian Americans.

Today, Italian Americans are integrated into U.S. society as white Americans. But that wasn't so in the early years of this century. People of southern Italian background were considered non-white well into the 1920s. We were called aliens, wops — meaning "without papers," just like today's undocumented immigrants. Nicola Sacco and Bartomoleo Vanzetti were derided as dagos, Reds and "anarchistic bastards" (by their trial judge, Webster Thayer). Anarchists were considered terrorists. Sound familiar?

When they were arrested and put on trial for murder, Sacco and Vanzetti got support from radical and genuinely democratic people of all nationalities and walks of life. Italian Americans who were poor, working class, new immigrants, much of the lower middle class, particularly identified with their suffering and stigmatization. My mother remembers her uncle saying: "Those men were murdered because they were Italian."

Sacco and Vanzetti themselves knew why they were being targeted. In Bartolomeo Vanzetti's words:

> I would not wish to a dog or to a snake what I have had to suffer for things that I am not guilty of. But my conviction is that I have suffered for things that I am guilty of. I am suffering because I am a radical and indeed I am a radical; I have suffered because I was an Italian, and indeed I am an Italian; I have suffered more for my family and my beloved than for myself; but I am so convinced to be right that if you could execute me two times, and if I could be reborn two other times, I would live again to do what I have done already.

Today, Sacco and Vanzetti are long dead and it's safe to feel sympathy for them. And many Italian Americans look back with nostalgia, from a comfortable position of white privilege, at this era when we actually were an oppressed national minority subject to persecution. But when Sacco and Vanzetti were facing execution and needing support, lots of Italian Americans — the establishment, some professionals, the wealthy — would have nothing to do with them. They didn't want to be associated with those radicals and "terrorists."

So I pose this challenge:

If you won't stand up now for the Arabs, Muslims and South Asians who are being held without any constitutional rights for supposed association with terrorists, you wouldn't have stood up for Sacco and Vanzetti either.

If you won't stand up for Mumia Abu-Jamal, the former Black Panther, journalist and exposer of the crimes of the Philadelphia Police Department who was railroaded and faces the death penalty for supposedly killing a Philadelphia police officer, you wouldn't have stood up for Sacco and Vanzetti either.

And if you won't stand up against Bush's endless war on whatever country is not bowing down to the dictates of the U.S. elite, you wouldn't have stood up for Sacco and Vanzetti either.

Nicola Sacco and Bartolomeo Vanzetti understood well that most wars are called by the rich to protect their wealth, their oil wells, their sources of profit. We shouldn't forget what they knew.

Long live the memory of Sacco and Vanzetti! Free the detainees! Free Mumia Abu-Jamal! Abolish the death penalty! No to Bush's war!

resources and further reading

AVRICH, PAUL. *Sacco and Vanzetti: The Anarchist Background.* (Princetown, New Jersey: Princetown University Press, 1991.)

FRANKFURTER, FELIX. *The Case of Sacco and Vanzetti: A Critical Analysis for Lawyers and Laymen.* (New York: Universal Library, 1962.)

PORTER, KATHERINE ANNE. *The Never-Ending Wrong.* (Boston: Little, Brown, 1977.)

SACCO, NICOLA and VANZETTI, BARTOLOMEO. *The Letters of Sacco and Vanzetti.* (New York: Octagon Books, 1971.)

cultural activism

GUTHRIE, WOODY.
    "Ballads of Sacco & Vanzetti." Commissioned by Moses Asch, 1945; composed and sung by Woody Guthrie, 1946-47.
    "Sacco's Letter to His Son." Sung by Pete Seeger. Folkways Records Album No. FH 5485, 1960.

MONTALDO, GIULIANO. "Sacco and Vanzetti." UMC Pictures, 1971. Theme song by Joan Baez, music written by Joan Baez and Ennio Morricone.

SHAHN, BEN. *The Passion of Sacco and Vanzetti.* 23 gouaches exhibited at the Downtown Gallery, New York, April 5-17, 1932.

SINCLAIR, UPTON. *Boston: A Documentary Novel of the Sacco-Vanzetti Case.* (Massachusetts: R.Bentley, 1978.)

WELLS, H.G. *The Way the World is Going.* (New York: Doubleday, Doran & Company, Inc., 1928.)

websites

The Sacco-Vanzetti Project (Harvard)
http://www.saccovanzettiproject.org/project.htm

Felix Frankfurter Essay on the Case (The Atlantic Monthly)
http://www.theatlantic.com/unbound/flashbks/oj/frankff.htm

Summary of Trial / Topical Cartoons
http://www.msu.edu/~brownse2/school/

radical history

POLITICS ON TRIAL
Five Famous Trials of the 20th Century
William Kunstler

Introduction by Karin Kunstler Goldman, Michael Ratner and Michael Steven Smith

William Kunstler, champion of civil liberties and human rights, reflects on five famous cases in which ordinary citizens were targeted for the color of their skin or the views they held.

Includes an essay on the case of Sacco and Vanzetti.

ISBN 1-876175-49-4

CHILE: THE OTHER SEPTEMBER 11
Commentaries and Reflections on the 1973 Coup in Chile
Edited by Pilar Aguilera and Ricardo Fredes

An anthology reclaiming September 11 as the anniversary of Pinochet's U.S.-backed coup in Chile, against the government of Salvador Allende. Contributors include Ariel Dorfman, Pablo Neruda, Víctor Jara, Joan Jara, Salvador Allende, Beatriz Allende and Fidel Castro.

ISBN 1-876175-50-8

ONE HUNDRED RED HOT YEARS
Big Moments of the 20th Century
Preface by Eduardo Galeano
Edited by Deborah Shnookal

A thrilling ride through the 20th century: 100 years of revolution, reaction and resistance.

ISBN 1-876175-48-6

rebel lives

helen keller

edited by John Davis

Poor little blind girl or dangerous radical? This book challenges the
sanitized image of Helen Keller, restoring her true history as a
militant socialist. Here are her views on women's suffrage, her
defense of the Industrial Workers of the World (IWW), her
opposition to World War I and her support for imprisoned socialist
and anarchist leaders, as well as her analysis of disability and class.

ISBN 1-876175-60-5

albert einstein

edited by Jim Green

You don't have to be Einstein... to know that he was a giant
in the world of science and physics. Yet this book takes a new,
subversive look at *Time* magazine's "Person of the Century," whose
passionate opposition to war and racism and advocacy of human
rights put him on the FBI's files as a socialist enemy of the state.

ISBN 1-876175-63-X

haydée santamaría

edited by Betsy Maclean

Haydée first achieved notoriety by being one of two women who
participated in the armed attack that sparked the Cuban Revolution.
Later, as director of the world-renowned literary institution, Casa de
las Americas, she embraced culture as a tool for social change and
provided refuge for exiled Latin American artists and intellectuals.

ISBN 1-876175-59-1

oceanpress

e-mail info@oceanbooks.com.au
www.oceanbooks.com.au